Peak District

Published by
The Horizon Press

Peak District

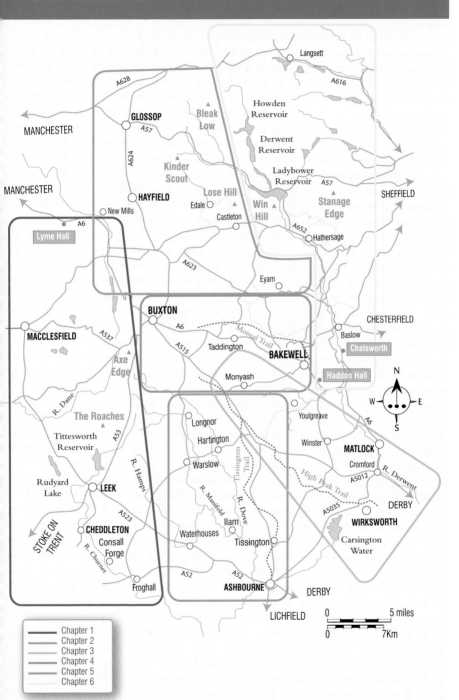

MANCHESTER

MANCHESTER

Langsett

A628

A616

GLOSSOP
A57

Bleak
Low

Howden
Reservoir

Derwent
Reservoir

A624

Kinder
Scout

Ladybower
Reservoir
A57

SHEFFIELD

New Mills

A6

HAYFIELD

Edale

Lose Hill

Castleton

Win
Hill

Stanage
Edge

Lyme Hall

A652

Hathersage

A623

Eyam

CHESTERFIELD

MACCLESFIELD

A537

BUXTON

A6

Monsal Trail

Baslow

Chatsworth

A515

Taddington

BAKEWELL

Axe
Edge

Monyash

Haddon Hall

R. Dane

The Roaches

Tittesworth
Reservoir

A53

Longnor

Hartington

Youlgreave

A6

Winster

MATLOCK

Rudyard
Lake

LEEK

R. Hamps

Warslow

Tissington Trail

R. Manifold

R. Dove

High Peak Trail

Cromford
A5012

R. Derwent

A523

Ilam

DERBY

STOKE ON TRENT

CHEDDLETON

Consall
Forge

R. Churnet

Waterhouses

Tissington

A5035

WIRKSWORTH

Carsington
Water

Froghall

A52

A52

ASHBOURNE

DERBY

LICHFIELD

N
W   E
S

0   5 miles
0   7Km

Chapter 1
Chapter 2
Chapter 3
Chapter 4
Chapter 5
Chapter 6

Contents

Feature Boxes

Top Tips

Chatsworth House/Garden and Standwood for bluebells

Visit Haddon Hall or Kedleston Hall

Lea Gardens near Lea for rhododendrons (over 500 species)

See the Well Dressing at either Bakewell, Tideswell, Tissington or Youlgreave

See Dovedale on a sunny summer morning

Visit Buxton for its fine buildings (my town guide available at the TIC)

Try the Scenic Route: Deep Valleys and High Moorlands p.160

Do a walk in the Upper Dane Valley/Wildboarclough area

For the kids – Go Ape! (Buxton); Alton Towers; Heights of Abraham

Bike ride (hire available) Waterhouses–Hulme End (Manifold Trail) or around Carsington Reservoir

Welcome to
The Peak District

The Peak District lies at the southern end of the Pennines surrounded by the cities of Sheffield to the north-east, Manchester to the north-west, Stoke-on-Trent to the south-west and Derby to the south-east. Although the Peak is often regarded as being wholly in Derbyshire, it must be remembered that large areas to the west are in Staffordshire – indeed Dovedale is

the county boundary here and some of the most spectacular scenery is on the Staffordshire bank – while west of Buxton a significant area of the Peak lies in Cheshire, with some areas to the north in South Yorkshire.

The rich diversity of scenery has long been an attraction for visitors, sufficient to move the hearts and pens of many nationally-known writers over the centuries. Nowadays, for convenience, the area is often sub-divided into the White Peak and the Dark Peak, each with its own quite distinct character.

The White Peak, defined very approximately as the countryside enclosed by the towns of Buxton, Castleton, Bakewell, Matlock, Ashbourne and Leek, is a limestone plateau of green fields and white stone walls. This upland is dissected by the rivers Derwent, Wye, Dove, Manifold and their tributaries to give the region's well-known dales, some with spectacular limestone rocks and cliffs. Dovedale, Manifold Valley, Chee Dale, Monsal Dale, Lathkill Dale and the Matlock Gorge are all deservedly popular beauty spots, while there are many more, lesser-known dales, many now 'dry' without their rippling trout streams, which are a delight to explore.

To the north and along the eastern and western margins of this limestone plateau lies the Dark Peak – upland areas of grassland, with moorlands covered with heather, bilberry and cotton grass, growing on gritstone and

Glutton Farm, Earl Sterndale

Monyash Welldressing

shale with a peaty acid soil, often a less hospitable area left to the sheep and grouse. This is the country loved by the rambler who wishes to 'get away from it all' and the rock gymnasts who delight in scaling the numerous gritstone 'edges'. Even this area is served by many minor roads, so that the less energetic can park easily and take a gentle stroll along the top of one of the edges with magnificent views over the surrounding countryside.

Couple all this with a rich historical background of stately homes, show caves, ancient lead mines, picturesque watermills, a network of old packhorse ways and numerous small towns and villages to explore, and it becomes clear why the Peak District is the most visited (some would say over-visited) national park in the western world.

Over-usage of places such as Dovedale, the Pennine Way path over Kinder Scout, and Stanage Edge caused erosion and the degeneration of paths to a point at which they became no longer acceptable to many visitors. Fortunately remedial action has resolved this. If this book succeeds in its aim of making visitors aware that there are other areas of equal importance and attractiveness, then its publication will be justified. Most country-lovers seek, or seem to seek, fine rural surroundings accompanied by a degree of solitude. One cannot over-stress that there are very many areas in the Peak where this can be achieved if one looks beyond such beauty spots as Dovedale.

Throughout this book, mention is made of the OS map, or Ordnance Survey Map to give its full title, and Grid Reference numbers. It is

essential to carry the maps called 'The White Peak' and 'The Dark Peak'. They contain such a wealth of information for visitors that they are indispensable. Do not be put off by thinking that you cannot read a map, for a little practice will show you how easy it really is.

A look at an atlas will show vividly the point made above relating to the geographical location of the Peak District National Park. The Park is unique in that its 555sq miles (1,440sq km) are surrounded by one conurbation after another. Over 17.5 million people live within 50 miles (81km) of the region and the Park attracts over 22 million visitors per year. This book is not, however, confined to a study of the Park itself. There are large areas of interest, such as the Churnet Valley, which are beyond its boundaries but are included here.

The Peak District National Park came into being as a result of the National Parks and Access to the Countryside Act of 1949. The National Park that was established differed from others (except the Lake District) in that it was vested with control over planning matters as well as having responsibility for providing information services to visitors. The policies of the Peak National Park Authority (referred to hereafter as the National Park) often conflict with the pressures of society, particularly industry, and restrictions on residential development have contributed to high property prices.

When combined with other factors such as the decline in economic importance of agriculture in the upland areas, the price of housing has resulted in a gradual depopulation of rural communities, particularly among young people. This vicious circle then makes schools redundant, and young people seek a life amongst their own age group in towns. There is no easy solution. The establishment of the National Park certainly came just at the right time, and its policies have been to our advantage. The Authority's vision statement: 'caring for a living landscape' sums up well its role.

The National Park also produces a considerable amount of literature on the area, much of it being for schools and some of it in French, Italian, Dutch and German. These leaflets are useful and informative both for adults and schoolchildren. They can be obtained directly from the National Park at Bakewell or from its information centres.

Among the wealth of other publications, four books stand out, being based upon original research and comprehensive in their approach. They are *The Peak District* by Millward and Robinson (Eyre Methuen); *The Peak District* by K C Edwards in the New Naturalist series, now a Fontana paperback; *Peakland Roads and Trackways* by A E & E M Dodd (Landmark Publishing Ltd); and *Wild Flowers and other plants of the Peak District* by Anderson and Shimwell, of which only the third is in print. Although there are of course definitive books on other disciplines such as geology, these four books are recommended for a good general background to the area.

There are plenty of walkers' guides to the Peak District. An attempt has been made to include a fair selection of walks in this book, which can easily be extended or shortened to suit

particular needs by using the OS map and following other rights of way. The 2.5in or 1:50,000 scale maps show every field. With the whole of the Peak almost entirely on two maps it is possible to sort out all manner of routes with comparative ease.

The Peak has been crossed by countless numbers of old roads and packhorse ways, which have now degenerated to bridle paths or footpaths. This is an important legacy which we are most fortunate to have. It means that we can leave the car and really get to know an area on paths now little used. Such is the network of paths that in some areas there is no difficulty in finding circular routes in order to return to the car. Good parking areas are provided in many places and are marked on the OS maps.

At this point perhaps one should stress a word of warning. The many old lead mines in the area present few problems to the rambler so long as they are avoided. On no account enter mine workings or caves without an expert, or remove the stones capping a shaft, or climb rock faces. The caving and mountain rescue posts were not established without good reason and a memorial at Castleton Youth Hostel to Neil Moss is a reminder that those who go underground do not always return. Rock faces and the northern moors have also claimed their share of lives.

Finally, please remember that, when the visitor has gone home, those living and working in the Peak will remain behind. Respect property and privacy, animals and crops and remember the adage: 'leave only footprints, take only photographs'; and have an enjoyable time.

The south-western edge of the Peak District is an area of open and often treeless moorland dissected by three river systems – the Churnet, Dane and Goyt. Flowing off the high moors, these three major valleys offer good walking and extensive views. There is much to see. The huge outcrops of rocks known as the Roaches are perhaps the most notable geographical feature. Man has however added much else – the two reservoirs of the Goyt Valley and one at Tittesworth, interesting market towns, preserved mills and the majestic Gothic Revival mansion of Alton Towers. One is tempted to single out particular parts of the valleys for special comment but this would perhaps be misleading, for all three are very attractive in their own particular way.

There are no contrasting features like those found in the valleys of the Dove and Manifold, for instance, where sandstones and shales give way to the harder limestone. Here, all the rocks are varieties of sandstone and shales. It is therefore a different kind of to-pography moulded in softer rock than the limestone, creating rugged heather and bilberry-clad moors in the upper valleys. Further downstream, wooded and often deep, wide valleys are more characteristic.

The Churnet rises to the east of the Roaches and Ramshaw Rocks, flowing into Tittesworth Reservoir. Standing on the road bridge at Meerbrook, over the northern end of Tittesworth Reser-voir, the water looks like a huge mirror for the Roaches escarpment behind.

To the east rises the ridge known as **Morridge**, with the Mermaid Inn standing out on the treeless skyline. Just to the north of the inn is **Blake-mere**, more popularly known as the **Mermaid Pool**, traditionally said to be bottomless and the home of a mermaid. It is strange that a pool very similar to this known as Doxey Pool also exists on the Roaches. The inn was on an old drover's road that ran from Cheshire into the Peak District via Hartington and Newhaven.

The Axe Edge moors afford good views over quite a large area. From the lay-by just south of the Mermaid Inn on Morridge one can, for instance, see to the Welsh Hills and the Wrekin in Shropshire on a clear day. The more

Park and ride

There is only limited parking on the narrow road that runs beneath the Roaches. However there is now a free park-and-ride scheme, which operates from **Tittesworth Reservoir** to the Roaches at week-ends. Vehicles are left at the Meerbrook end, where there is a modern visitor centre close to the Meerbrook-Blackshaw Moor road. There is also a café, children's play area, sensory garden and an interactive water exhibition. Severn Trent Water organize regular special events.

immediate view down to the Roaches and Ramshaw Rocks is perhaps more spectacular. If your route takes you up the Leek-Buxton road past **Ramshaw Rocks,** drive slowly looking for the rock which obviously resembles a face. Known as the **Winking Eye** rock, it does just that as you drive past it.

Below Tittesworth Reservoir, the river skirts the old market town of Leek. The river has for centuries been used for power and for its very pure qualities. The Cistercian monks built one of the largest abbey churches of their order in England on the banks of the River Churnet at Abbey Green, Leek and also established a watermill, presumably to grind corn. The abbey is no more, but a preserved corn mill still stands on the site of the original mill.

At Leek, the river sweeps in a huge arc around the town, meandering out almost to Rudyard where it flows back towards the town in a very deep valley carved out by overflow waters from a glacial lake, known as Lake Dane, that was situated just to the north of Rudyard Lake. A good place to view this is from the Leek to Stoke-on-Trent road (the A53) where it crosses the river. Below Cheddleton, where another preserved watermill exists, the valley is well wolton village where it becomes shallower. This section is perhaps the prettiest part of the valley due to the lack of roads. Instead it is traversed by railway and canal, the latter adding to the tranquil atmosphere.

The valley of the River Dane is similar to the Churnet in that motor traffic is denied access to much of it. The river rises on Axe Edge above Three Shires Head and flows roughly westwards to the Cheshire plain where it meanders slowly towards the River Weaver. It has a tributary, the Clough Brook, which collects the waters from the Wildboarclough district; this is another large and beautiful valley or 'clough' worth exploring.

The valleys of the Dane and Clough Brook were important to the laden packhorses which crossed the southern Pennines carrying salt to the east of England. An interesting feature of Three Shires Head − where the counties of Cheshire, Derbyshire and Staffordshire meet − are the many packhorse routes that converge at Panniers Pool.

Lud Church

Lower downstream near Gradbach, a huge landslip has created a gorge of considerable proportions high on the hillside. Known as Lud Church, this is well worth the effort of getting to. In excess of 50ft (15m) deep and in places only a few feet wide, it became a meeting place of religious dissidents some 500 years ago and supposedly takes its name from their leader.

Above Lud Church and Back Forest in which it is situated, various paths cut through the heather and bilberry amid the exposed gritstone rock. This is the home of the grouse and curlew, disturbed only by the rambler enjoying the magnificent scenery. Below Danebridge, a road crosses the valley, making this a good starting place to explore the area. After a few miles it widens out and ends abruptly under the shadow of Bosley Cloud, a huge outcrop of harder gritstones.

The Goyt starts close to the Dane in the wide expanse of peat bogs north of Three Shires Head. Once the tree line is reached the valley becomes of more interest, but its physical character is lost beneath the waters of Fernilee and Errwood reservoirs. To the west rises Shining Tor and the exposed edge of gritstone known as Windgather Rocks. Despite much of it being flooded, there is plenty of interest in the Goyt Valley.

Historical remains

Compared with other areas of the Peak, there is not a great deal remaining of early occupation in this area. A notable exception is the prehistoric burial mound known as the **Bridestones**, situated at the southern end of the large hill, **Bosley Cloud**, close to the Congleton-Rushton-Leek road. It is a chambered burial tomb with some very tall standing stones. Visible from the road, it is accessible to the public and well worth examining. While parked by the Bridestones, look out to the west. On a clear day one can see the Welsh Hills and much nearer, **Jodrell Bank Radio Telescope** in Cheshire, which has an impressive visitor centre and a large arboretum.

Dieulacresse Abbey at Leek has been completely destroyed except for a small part of a pillar, but of comparable age is the town's parish church, which is well worth a visit. The church of St Edward the Confessor at Leek was founded in 1042. It has a beautiful pair of 13th-century rose windows and some ancient crosses in the churchyard. Despite alterations over nearly a thou-

sand years, much of interest remains of the old church. A guide book is on sale in the vestry.

Two churches of similar age to Leek are at Cheddleton and Horton, situated about 4 miles (6km) south and west of Leek respectively. Further north Rushton church, situated in the fields halfway between Rushton James and Rushton Spencer so as to serve both villages, is well worth a visit, as is the Forest Chapel north of Wildboarclough which was erected in 1673 and rebuilt in 1834. Here the annual rush laying ceremony in August can be observed.

The **Roman Catholic Church at Cheadle**, Staffordshire, built during 1840-6 and considered to be the finest Revival Gothic church in the country, is a MUST. It was designed by A W N Pugin while enjoying the patronage and friendship of the Earl of Shrewsbury, who paid £40,000 for its construction. Incongruously situated off the main street, its huge spire overshadows the town. Its richly painted interior is a not-to-be-overlooked visit.

The Churnet Valley

The water of the valley spawned textile industries, which developed to take advantage of its power and purity. **Leek** developed as a textile town producing silk. Dyestuffs were produced in great quantities, particularly in the 19th century when it was found that the water could be used to produce the raven-black dyes for which the town became so famous and which were so popular with the Victorians. Old textile mills mingle with silk workers' houses, but none are open to the public.

The town is well-known for its

St Giles, Roman Catholic Church, Cheadle

The Caldon Canal, Consall Forge

The South West

Stockport

Lyme Hall

Bugsworth

Whaley Bridge

Chapel-en-le-Frith

A6

Adlington Hall

N
W — E
S

Fernilee
Reservoir

0   1   2 miles

0   1km

B5470

MACCLESFIELD

Jenkin
Chapel

Errwood
Reservoir

BUXTON

A537

A536

A6

Tegg's Nose

Forest Chapel

Cat &
Fiddle Inn

A515

Gawsworth Hall

Wildboarclough

A54

Three Shires
Head

Flash

A523

Danebridge

Gradbach

Lud Church

Longnor

Ramshaw
Rocks

Hartington

Rushton Spencer

Warslow

R. Dove

Bridestones

Tittesworth
Reservoir

A53

Rudyard
Lake

B5053

Brindley Mill

LEEK

Onecote

Alstonfield

B523

Flint
Mill

Coombes
Valley

B5053

R. Manifold

A515

Deep Hayes

Cheddleton

Railway
Museum

Consall
Forge

R. Churnet

Ipstones

Waterhouses

Stoke on Trent

B5053

Consall
Nature
Centre

Froghall

Whiston

Cauldon Lowe

A52

ASHBOURNE

B5417

Foxfield
Light Railway

Oakamoor

B5032

CHEADLE

Rambler's
Retreat

Alton
Towers

Alton

Norbury

markets and antique shops. There are indoor markets on Wednesday and Saturday and an outdoor collectables and craft market on a Saturday. Outdoors on Wednesday there is a busy general market and on Saturday an antiques, collectables and craft market. There are several galleries including the **Moorland Arts and Antiques Centre** housed in Cross Street Mill. Also in this converted mill building is **Kiddies Kingdom** an indoor play area for young children, perfect for letting off steam on a wet day.

A walk around Leek's main streets reveals the Victorian influence particularly under the design of the Sugdens, a local firm of architects. In the Market Place is a Butter Cross, dating from 1671. The town's **cornmill in Mill Street** has been preserved and is worth a visit. It is claimed by enthusiasts to have been built by James Brindley, who had his workshops in the town. The waterwheel and all its machinery are intact and in working condition and the second floor has been developed as a museum to Brindley. Although better known as a canal engineer, his early career was as a millwright.

Visitors are welcome at the RSPB **Coombes Valley Nature Reserve**, which protects woodland and pasture in the Coombes Valley, a tributary of the Churnet, between Cheddleton and Ipstones near to Leek. This can be approached from the A52 Leek to Ashbourne road and a few miles further along this road is the **Blackbrook Zoological Park**. A large and varied collection of some of the most rare and endangered species in the world are housed here with birds a particular speciality. The zoo is involved in a number of breeding programmes helping to save rare species from extinction.

At **Cheddleton** on the A520 south of Leek is a preserved **flint grinding mill**. The picturesque site is adjacent to the Caldon Canal and a preserved narrow boat is moored here. Flint stones were calcined in kilns and ground to powder, then used in the Potteries to make bone china, hence its local importance. With two working waterwheels, the mill has become an important tourist attraction where the whole process is demonstrated.

At Cheddleton, the old railway station about a mile downstream from the mill can be visited. It has a collection of steam locomotives and rolling stock and a museum devoted to the **North Staffordshire Railway**. From the station the **Churnet Valley Railway** runs steam and diesel serv-

Double sunset

An interesting phenomenon is sometimes observed from St. Edward's churchyard Leek, from the 20-22 June each year. At this time, if conditions are satisfactory, the setting sun will be seen completely to set behind Bosley Cloud. If atmospheric conditions are right, the sun can be seen to reappear from the side of Bosley Cloud's distinctive escarpment and finally set over the Cheshire plain. The double sunset can never be guaranteed because of cloud on the horizon, but many go to watch this spectacle each year.

ices over a 10.5 mile (17km) stretch of restored track through the valley to Froghall. A new station and visitor centre has been built at Froghall. Trains run most weekends and some weekdays in high season. Passengers can alight at Consall or Froghall and walk back to Cheddleton along the Caldon Canal or simply enjoy a picnic and catch a later service back.

A little further south at the **Foxfield Steam Railway** near to Dilhorne, just off the Cheadle to Stoke-on-Trent road, you can take a ride on a steam train for a few miles along a restored colliery line. Special events take place throughout the year.

The main appeal of the Churnet lies below Cheddleton, where the valley bottom can be followed along the canal towpath to Froghall. If you are particularly interested in canals and their architecture, take your car to Denford, just off the Leek to Hanley road (A53) at Longsdon. Walk westwards past the canal-side pub (the Hollybush) under the aqueduct, which carries the Leek arm of the canal, to **Hazelhurst locks**. There is a canal keeper's cottage, a fine cast-iron footbridge and much to interest the photographer.

Parking is difficult in Denford and an alternative way to explore that part of the canal and to enjoy some lovely countryside is to park at **Deep Hayes Country Park,** which is close by. It is then a short walk to The Hollybush and the locks.

The Cheddleton to Froghall section really starts at Basford Bridge near the railway station. The valley is well wooded and the leafy glades provide a marvellous backcloth for the canal. **Consall Forge**

is a small hamlet on the canal. Steep steps descend from each side of the valley to reach it, giving a more direct access than along the canal towpath. The hamlet gets its name from an old iron forge, which existed in Elizabethan times, but all trace of it has long gone. Here, the canal and river run in one channel – a broad expanse of slow-moving water, which separates again in front of the old canal pub, the Black Lion – now a very popular inn serving good food.

The canal disappears under a footbridge and the railway, to meander casually down to Froghall and the wharf there. The river commences its own course once more at the foot of a large weir and the whole scene is worth stopping to examine and photograph. Look out also for the remains of the huge lime kilns near to the canal. There is a **Nature Centre** situated on the road between Consall and Consall Forge.

Below Consall Forge is the former Podmore's Flint Mill, the last surviving local flint crushing mill serving the pottery industry. Two and a half miles (4km) further on is **Froghall** with its vast copper works and canal wharf. Here a picnic area has been created at the canal basin, and one can explore the old limekilns and loading docks where limestone was loaded onto railway wagons or into narrow boats. The quarry wagons ran on a 3ft 6in (1.07m) gauge track and lengths of rail of this gauge remain. With the 2ft 6in (0.76m) gauge of the Manifold Valley Light Railway, the North Staffordshire Railway was the only railway company in Britain to have lines of three different gauges.

The incline to the quarry at Cauldon

A winter's day on the Caldon Canal

Walks in the Churnet Valley

There are a variety of walks, which enable the valley to be seen at its best, particularly as the beauty spots are, for the most part, denied to the motorist. The canal towpath from Froghall, where there is a picnic site, can be used to gain access to Consall Forge. Alternatively there are two paths that descend more directly to the hamlet. The towpath from Froghall, as distinct from the path from Cheddleton which can be muddy, is fit for wheelchairs, although there is a bridge with steps to cross.

The more direct paths descend to the Churnet from Consall village and from Belmont. In each case there are numerous steps to descend but Consall Forge is well worth the effort. Park in Consall village and walk eastwards towards the valley. At a bend in the road, a signpost to Consall Forge indicates the start of a well-used path which crosses fields before descending into the valley for 1.5 miles (2km).

The more interesting route to the river is from Belmont pools, down the 'Devil's Staircase'. The 200 steps descend from the wood near Belmont pools through the estate of Belmont Hall (not open to the public). Park with care (the road is very narrow) at Belmont pools on the Cheddleton to Ipstones road. The path (not the hall drive) is taken to Consall Forge. The pools are popular with photographers – the huge beech trees create a perfect setting for the artificial pools. By the road here is an old chapel which was built for his private use when the owner of the hall fell out with the vicar of Ipstones. It has been carefully restored but, like the hall, it is a private residence not open to the public.

St Edward's Parish Church, Leek

Cheddleton flint mill

Alton Towers

Situated at Alton, 3 miles (5km) east of Cheadle, this huge mansion, formerly home of the Earls of Shrewsbury is today a gutted shell but the grounds have been developed as, arguably, the UK's if not Europe's premier theme park. With over 120 rides, including 'Air' and 'Nemesis', and the world's largest log flume 2600ft (792m) in length, it has something for everyone. There are two hotels on site, one of which opens in June 2003, and these give access to the Cariba Water Park, full of amazing 'splash fun' for all the family.

Of particular interest are the gardens, once noted as the largest domestic gardens in Europe, and especially lovely in May when the rhododendrons flower. Around the valley there are many paths and steps, a corkscrew fountain, a Gothic temple, a Swiss Chalet, a huge range of conservatories and much use of water. In the summer the band plays in the bandstand and over the tree tops water shoots into the sky from the 'Chinese Pagoda' fountain, its gold painted bells glistening through the falling water.

Alton Towers is a big place, attracting large crowds so go early in the morning. It will be quieter mid-week. A single entrance fee covers all rides and there are over 50 catering outlets, free parking and facilities for disabled people.

It is open from the first weekend in April (earlier if Easter is earlier) until the first weekend in November, daily from 9.30am-5.30pm.
☎ 08705 420 4060 for bookings. www.altontowers.com

Low was the second oldest tramway in the country, dating from 1777. If you are in Froghall with a car, take the Kingsley road and take the first turn right along a narrow lane that gives several views down into the valley, if time does not permit a walk. It eventually passes a footpath marked 'Consull' [sic]. A quarter of a mile walk down here gives further excellent views into the valley and access to the canal towpath at Podmore's Flint Mill.

On Sundays a canal boat with crew in period costume operates from Froghall Wharf, offering a cruise with lunch or afternoon tea. Book beforehand if possible as it is very popular. Now that the Churnet Valley Railway runs to Froghall it might be possible to arrive by train, cruise the canal and return by train at the end of the day. Careful studying of the timetables is advised.

Although the valley between Froghall and **Oakamoor** is denied even to the rambler, the latter village is worth investigation. It has two old pubs and a picnic site on the foundations of an old copper works, demolished in 1963 and now consolidated at Froghall. Here Messrs Thomas Bolton & Sons manufactured the copper wire core for the first transatlantic cable in 1856.

Other than a few date stones, nothing now remains of the works except for a very large mill pool, the retained water cascading down a stepped weir before disappearing under the road bridge.

The **Hawksmore Nature Reserve** near Oakamoor, on the road to Cheadle welcomes visitors. It is owned by the National Trust and a trail has been laid out in the extensive grounds which drop towards the Churnet.

The section of valley between Oakamoor and Alton offers a choice of routes. The road via Farley leaves the valley, affording views of the latter and the Weaver Hills. It goes through Farley village with its attractive cottages and beautiful hall, once the home of the Bill family. Beyond Farley, the views are towards Alton Towers, its turrets soaring above the trees. The more direct route to Alton keeps to the valley bottom. On reaching the former Pink Lodge, now a café and restaurant, one can walk westwards up Dimmingsdale to the former mill and its beautiful pools beyond. The café, now known as **The Rambler's Retreat Coffee House**, (☎ 01538 702730) is very popular in what used to be quite a quiet, secluded area. There is a large car park for visitors to Dimmingsdale adjacent to the café.

The old mill was built in the eighteenth century as a lead smelter. It has been converted to a dwelling house with the pitwheel and wallower preserved, although the external wheel remains in need of restoration. There are paths up Dimmingsdale on either side of the pools behind the mill; it is possible to cross the valley, so making a short circular walk. This area is well wooded and is particularly beautiful in the autumn when the leaves turn red or yellow prior to falling.

Opposite the Rambler's Retreat, a little unsurfaced lane runs down to the river and former railway (now a cycle path from Oakamoor to Alton). The bridge over the latter used to be a popular spot for photographing the steam trains, which ran down the valley prior to the Beeching closures. The lane itself is part of the Earl's Drive, which went from Alton Towers, up Dimmingsdale and on towards Cheadle. It enabled the Earl to get most of the way to Cheadle – entirely on his own land!

Alton village once enjoyed the patronage of the Earls of Shrewsbury who owned almost everything in the area. Look out for the village lock-up and the castle. The valley bottom at Alton has much to offer. The view up to the castle, perched high on the rocks above, looks like a Rhineland replica. The old railway station, built by Pugin (who also designed the Catholic church at Cheadle) has been restored, while opposite is an old watermill. It is difficult to imagine that this old mill was once a copper and brass wire mill, producing 'Guinea-rods' in huge quantities as currency for the African slave trade. Look out for the lodge to the Towers, also attributed to Pugin.

If you are standing near to the lodge above the old railway station (restored by the Landmark Trust), look over to your left. The outline of the old millpond can be seen. It was narrowed to make way for the Froghall – Uttoxeter branch of the Caldon Canal, but the latter was later filled in and used as the trackbed of the railway. Some long stretches of the canal exist between

Lud Church, Gradbach

The River Dane at Gradbach

View from Shuttlingsloe

Three Shires Head, Dane Valley

Alton and Denstone old railway line between Oakamoor and Denstone is now a cycle track.

The Dane and Upper Goyt Valleys

The Dane Valley, with its tributary the Clough Brook, rivals the Churnet and Dove Valleys as a major beauty spot in the west of the Peak District. Rising on Whetstone Edge, close to the Cat and Fiddle Inn, its deeply-cut valley confines the infant waters of the river. Using old packhorse routes as paths it is possible to walk down much of the valley. The old bridge at **Three Shires Head** should not be missed. Have a look underneath it to see that the bridge has been widened at some

Walks in the Dane Valley

The area around Three Shires Head has several old packhorse routes which can be used for exploration. The one from Flash Bar (i.e. the Travellers Rest pub at SK032679) via Drystone Edge and Blackclough can be used for wheelchairs, if you do not mind the path being a little rough in places. It has a tarmac or stone surface for much of its way, but is not open to motor vehicles. You may return by Turn Edge to make a 5 mile (8km) circular route although this is not recommended for wheelchairs.

A recommended 9 mile (14.5km) circular route takes in the Dane and Clough Brook. For convenience, start at Wildboarclough where there is adequate roadside parking. Just upstream of the Crag Inn take the footbridge over the brook and climb over the hill to the main road (A54) and Tagsclough Hill. From here, this old packhorse route continues straight to Gradbach Mill via Burntcliff Top. It emerges at the Flash to Allgreave road by the side of an old pub, the Eagle and Child, now a private house. Inside the entrance is a plaque depicting an eagle and child taken from the arms of the Stanleys, Earls of Derby, who own Crag Hall and its estate at Wildboarclough. From Gradbach Mill proceed upstream to the chapel where a path cuts up the hill east of the Dane to Turn Edge where it meets the packhorse route to Three Shires Head from Flash. Cross the bridge at Three Shires Head and continue over to Cumberland Brook via Holt Farm and the western edge of Dane Bower. Follow the brook down to the road and turn downstream to Wildboarclough.

North of the Dane the upper Goyt down to Errwood Reservoir makes an interesting 3 mile (5km) walk, and time should be allowed to explore the ruins of Errwood Hall and its grounds. Cars must be parked at Derbyshire Bridge (SK 017718) or at the car park (The Street) on the hillside above the dam between the two reservoirs. If you visit the area midweek and drive from Pym Chair, or the east side of the valley, you can drive down to Errwood and out via Derbyshire Bridge.

time either for increased horse traffic or for the passage of carts.

A couple of miles downstream from the bridge is **Gradbach**, a scattered community with no village as such. It is easily approached off the A53 – the Leek to Buxton road – through **Flash**, which at 1,525ft (469m) is the highest village in England. This is a harsh village of weather worn cottages, huddled together on the side of Oliver Hill. Descending down to the Dane, the scenery is more interesting and the climate more tolerant.

Gradbach is worth taking time to explore. Lacking a village centre, it is best to park at the car park on the lane to the youth hostel and by the side of the river. Look out for the old Methodist Chapel, built in 1849, and the adjacent cottage by the bridge over the river Dane, before walking downstream towards Gradbach Mill and Back Forest. The mill is easy to find, simply take the road to Flash from the bridge and turn first right down the side of a small brook. This is however a narrow road; once the car park is reached it is better to park there and walk.

Gradbach Mill, now owned by the Youth Hostels Association, used to be a silk mill with a large waterwheel fed by water from the Dane. It was rebuilt in 1758 following a fire, and closed down as a silk mill about 100 years later. Its large waterwheel was scrapped in the 1950s.

A good example of an old packhorse road can be seen ascending the hill on the opposite side of the river from the mill. Below the mill lies **Lud Church** and **Back Forest**, a large wood, which was stripped of its main timber in the mid-1950s. Lud Church (SJ987657) has already been mentioned, but it is worth repeating that it repays a visit, preferably on a walk from Gradbach by way of **Hanging Stone** to Danebridge and Swythamley, a distance of approximately 8 miles (13km). Much of the area south of the river between Gradbach and Danebridge formed part of the Swythamley Estate, which was divided and sold in 1977. The estate also included Swythamley Hall, plus the Roaches. The latter were purchased in 1980 by the National Park at a cost of £185,000.

If the walk mentioned above is taken, stop near the Hanging Stone. The view over Swythamley and south-eastwards towards the Roaches is worth more than a passing glance. Indeed, before coming over the bluff from Gradbach, the view northwards up to the Clough Brook with the high hill of **Shutlingsloe** rising to 1,659ft (506m) is even more interesting. The Hanging Stone carries two plaques, one to a pet dog, the other to the brother of the last Brocklehurst of Swythamley. He was Lieutenant Colonel Brocklehurst, an ex-gamewarden in the Sudan who established a private zoo on the Roaches, which included deer, a kangaroo, wallabies and a yak. Descendants of the deer still roam these hills. On reaching Danebridge take the well-defined path, which starts by the side of the bridge, back to Gradbach through the fields above the River Dane.

Further north under the hill of Shutlingsloe lies **Wildboarclough**. Taking the road westwards from Gradbach a couple of miles brings one to Allgreave where the minor road joins the A54.

Turn right on the main road for about half a mile (800m) and the sign on the left will point the way to **Hilly Billy Ice Cream Farm** where visitors can learn about a working hill farm whilst enjoying the tea room or sampling delicious home-made ice cream.

Just beyond the Clough Brook a minor road turns off to the right to run northwards towards Shutlingsloe. This road hugs the brook all the way to Wildboarclough. It is an attractive route and passes the Crag Inn, a popular stopping-off place for visitors. The village boasted the largest sub-post office in England before it closed. This distinction arises from the post office being in what was the administration block of a now demolished textile mill. Traces of the mill can be seen from the road at the T-junction just up river from the Crag Inn.

On the hillside above the post office is Crag Hall, the country seat of Lord Derby. Above the hall in the lane that leads northwards towards Bottom-of-the-Oven, look for the five horse troughs laid out in a semicircle. The roadway near the hall abounds with rhododendrons, which are a riot of colour in early summer. If time permits, continue upstream for half a mile (800m) or so and leave the car where the signpost indicates the path to Cumberland Brook. Walk up the brook past the deep ravine, with its rushing white water and dark conifers, to the waterfall before returning to the car.

Just above **Danebridge** the waters of the Clough and Dane unite to form a good sized river flowing beneath the broad arch after which the village takes its name. Like many neighbouring communities, Danebridge consists of a few loosely grouped cottages. It also has an interesting old pub, the Ship Inn, which until recently had some relics of Bonnie Prince Charlie's 1745 uprising, including a flintlock of a Scottish soldier and part of a newspaper he was carrying. The name Ship Inn is said to be a reminder of the *S S Swithamley* [sic], although the present inn sign is of the *Nimrod,* which took Shackleton, and Sir Phillip Brocklehurst of Swythamley, to the Antarctic.

The broad fields below Danebridge, broken by areas of woodland and views of Bosley Cloud, make a pleasant walk to Gig Hall Bridge, where the feeder channel to Rudyard reservoir starts. Above the valley is Wincle Grange Farm where the monks of old had a sheep and cattle farm. Further north, connected by a track to the grange, is Cleulow Cross, now hidden by the trees that surround it. It was probably a waymark cross on the route to the coast from Dieulacresse Abbey at Leek, which had important holdings of sheep and is known to have exported wool to Italy.

From Gig Hall Bridge, the feeder supply winds down the valley to Rushton. It has a path at the side, much in the nature of a towpath, which provides a pleasant walk. Below the village lies **Rudyard Lake**, built in 1797 by John Rennie as a water supply to the Trent and Mersey Canal and today a popular resort for visitors. The Rudyard Lake Steam Railway runs from here. A new visitor centre has been built which with facilities for fishing, boating, picnics, birdwatching and walking offers something for everyone. In case

View towards The Roaches

Jenkin Chapel, west of the Goyt Valley and Pym Chair

you have been wondering, Rudyard Kipling was named after the lake; his parents met here.

North of the Dane lies **Macclesfield Forest**, the high moorland of **Shining Tor** and the **Goyt**. The road upstream from Wildboarclough can be used as a good introduction to the area. Turn first left (above the village, opposite Dryknowle Farm). The road soon enters the forest to pass between Trentabank and Ridgegate Reservoirs. Upon reaching **Trentabank Reservoir** there is a visitor centre, car park, toilets, several woodland trails and a large heronry. At the road junction opposite the pub turn right, up the narrow road which climbs steeply uphill.

The narrow road climbs up to the hamlet of Macclesfield Forest with its rugged chapel and school. The Forest chapel, a low and simple building with an equally small bell tower, is well known for its Rush Bearing Service. On the nearest Sunday to 12 August, the chapel floor is strewn with rushes and a service is held in the afternoon, attended by many people. South-west of the chapel and north of the road to Langley is an earthwork, roughly rectangular and consisting of a rampart and ditch. Excavations have revealed foundations of a building considered to be the original hunting lodge of the old forest.

Continue to Bottom-of-the-Oven and then drive up the lane northwards to **Lamaload Reservoir**. It has a picnic area at its northern end, which is a quieter stopping place than at Errwood Reservoir, in the Goyt Valley.

Just beyond Lamaload Reservoir, the road divides, the right hand fork going to Jenkin Chapel (see below). The left hand fork goes to Rainow and, after a few yards, passes an intriguing memorial stone at the side of the road. The inscription reads: 'Here John Turner was cast away in a heavy snow storm in the night in or about the year 1755'. On the reverse side it reads 'The print of a woman's shoe was found by his side in the snow were [sic] he lay dead'.

From Lamaload proceed to **Jenkin Chapel**, which according to the tablet, was built at John Slack's expense in 1733. The short tower was added in 1755. The chapel looks more like a house than a religious building, and even the interior has a homely feel about it with its compactness and box pews. It was built alongside an important saltway. Just to the south is Saltersford Hall, a reminder of the days when pack horses with panniers loaded with salt made their way towards the Peak. An open air service is held here on the second Sunday in September at 3pm.

Turn eastwards and climb over **Pym Chair** before dropping down to the twin reservoirs of **Errwood** and **Fernilee**. The former rivals Rudyard Lake and there is a picnic site overlooking the water. The ruins of Errwood Hall near the south-western end of the water are an interesting detour, particularly when the rhododendrons are in bloom. When the reservoir was being built, the old packhorse bridge known as Derbyshire Bridge was moved upriver. A gunpowder works used to operate nearby many years ago. There are two picnic areas by Errwood Reservoir, one in the wood at the Errwood end of the road from Jenkin Chapel and the other at the upper end of the reservoir close to the ruins of Errwood Hall. A forest trail links up with this picnic area. This area is very popular when the rhododendrons are in flower. Yachting takes place on Errwood Reservoir.

The Goyt can be left by crossing the dam. The steep inclined road was formerly part of the Cromford and High Peak Railway and wagons used to be hauled up the incline by a steam engine at the top. The reservoir at the top of the incline provided water for the engine's boiler.

Alternatively take the one-way road up Goyt's Clough past **Goytsclough Quarry**, where there are more picnic tables. It reaches **Derbyshire Bridge** to meet an old road known as Jagger's Gate. To the west on the open moorland is the **Cat and Fiddle Inn**, built in 1831. Second to Tan Hill, it is the highest pub in England, standing at 1,690ft (515m) above sea level. Just beyond it on the Macclesfield side, an old coach road, turnpiked in 1759, goes off to the right. It is known as Stoneyway and retains its original surface. A short distance from the current road is a milestone reading 'To London 164 miles'. The road was abandoned in 1823 when the turnpike was realigned.

Macclesfield and around

Macclesfield is an old textile town which expanded following the building of the Macclesfield Canal and later the railway. Of particular interest to visitors are the **Silk Museum and Heritage Centre** – the first museum in Britain to be devoted to the silk industry. Housed in the former Sunday School, it includes a restored Victorian classroom. Nearby **Paradise Mill** may dispute the Silk Mill and Heritage Centre's claim to fame, for it is a working museum of the town's former silk industry. Twenty-six hand-powered Jacquard looms survive and practical demonstrations are given.

Away from the silk industry Macclesfield also has the **West Park Museum,** which houses a small but important collection of Egyptian antiquities. Natural history lovers will appreciate seeing some early works by Charles Tunnicliffe who was born locally.

Between Macclesfield and Macclesfield Forest is the **Tegg's Nose Country Park**, based around an old sandstone quarry. A static exhibit about the quarry uses some of the original equipment, and there are various walks, which start from the car park. Another walk is the Middlewood Way, a reclaimed railway line 11 miles (17.7km) long between Macclesfield and Middlewood, which is useful for cycling and horse riding, or it can be used as part of a circular path incorporating the Macclesfield Canal or the Gritstone Trail.

The Gritstone Trail is a 20 mile (32km) path from Lyme Park near Disley, to Rushton near Leek. It links with the **Staffordshire Way** to make a long distance path and passes through Tegg's Nose Country Park. A leaflet about the trail is available from nearby tourist information centres. Both these trails have memorable views in almost all directions.

The Macclesfield area has several country houses open to the public. **Adlington Hall** to the north dates mainly from the 15th century, with a Regency south front. It is a beautiful half-timbered house set in fine grounds. The great hall is a particularly interesting survival, while the Georgian barn is now a tea room.

West of Macclesfield is **Capesthorne Hall**, with a massive front longer than Buckingham Palace. Its central portion was rebuilt by Salvin after a disastrous fire in the 19th century. South of the town is **Gawsworth Hall**, a serene place which dates from 1480, although part of it was demolished in 1701 when the house was remodelled.

At the northern extremity of this area, and right on the edge of the conurbation south of Manchester, is **Lyme Hall** on the A6 near Disley, 6.5 miles (10km) south of Stockport. It was built in Elizabethan times and enlarged in the 18th and 19th centuries. This large house, now owned by the National Trust, has a Palladian south front reminiscent of Chatsworth's west front, gardens and a large deer park.

Inside there is fine furniture and one of the most important collections of early English clocks outside London.

Lyme Hall featured in the TV adaptation of Jane Austen's *Pride and Prejudice*. The drive and south front were used for shooting scenes of Pemberley, Mr Darcy's house. It was here that Colin Firth emrged from a swim in the lake to meet Elizabeth Bennet. The garden, pool and south front were clearly recognisable. Lyme has a lot to offer and it is well worth allocating a day there, whether you wish to walk in the park, explore the house or its lovely gardens.

Jane Austen – who lived in Hampshire – came to Derbyshire in 1806. The trip to Derbyshire made by Elizabeth Bennet was based upon the author's own journey, as indeed was Jane Eyre's journey based upon a similar visit by Charlotte Bronte. *Jane Eyre* was recently filmed at Haddon Hall and around Hathersage, where much inspiration for the novel originated.

Lyme Hall with the lake from which Mr Darcy emerged in Jane Austin's 'Pride and Prejudice', filmed by the BBC

Places to Visit

Tittesworth Reservoir

Meerbrook, 4 miles (6.5km) north of Leek ST13 8SW
☎ 01538 300400
www.st.water.co.uk/tittesworth
Open all year except Christmas Day. Walks around the reservoir, play area, visitor centre, café, scented garden and parking for Roaches' park and ride service. Free entry

Jodrell Bank Science Centre, Planetarium and Arboretum

Macclesfield, Cheshire Off A535 near Holmes Chapel SK11 9DL
☎ 01477 571339
www.manchester.ac.uk/jodrellbank/viscen
Open: 10.30am-5.00pm daily, Mar–Oct; other times vary
See the giant radio telescope at close quarters, learn about space and the environment. View the heavens in the planetarium and enjoy a stroll through the arboretum. Café and shop.
® & ♔<16 great for kids ☂

Leek

Moorland Arts and Antiques Centre

Cross Street Mill, Cross Street
☎ 01538 399210
Open: Mon–Sat 10am–5pm; Sundays and Bank Holidays 10am–4pm

Leaps and Bounds

Cross Street Mill ST13 6BL
☎ 01538 382333
Open: Daily, 10am–6.30pm. Closed Tue, term time.
Indoor play centre for small children
♔ ☂

Brindley Water Mill

Mill Street
☎ 01538 483741
Open: Easter-Sep, weekends and Bank Holiday Mondays, 2–5pm; late July and Aug, also Mon, Tue and Wed 2–5pm.

Operational cornmill. Museum of the life and times of James Brindley, engineer 1716-72.

Coombes Valley Nature Reserve

Six Oaks Farm, Nr Apesford, ST13 7EU
Off A523 Ashbourne to Leek road
☎ 01538 384017
www.rspb.org.uk/coombesvalley
Open: Daily 9am–9pm (or dusk). Free entry. Visitor centre open daily 9am–5pm.
® ♔ free

Blackbrook Zoological Park

Winkhill, off A523 south of Leek ST13 7QR
☎ 01538 308293
www.blackbrookzoo.co.uk
Open: 10.30am–5.30pm, summer (dusk in winter).
Collection of birds and animals, many endangered species. Tea room, shop.
® & ♔<17

Churnet Valley

Cheddleton Flint Mill

Cheadle Rd, Cheddleton, Leek ST13 7HL
☎ 0161 408 5083
www.ex.ac.uk/~akoutram/cheddleton-mill
Open: Wed, Sat and Sun 1–4.30pm, most weekends 10.30am–5pm, closed Christmas and New Year.
Watermill which tells the story of preparation of materials for the pottery industry. Free entry.
® & ♔ free ☂

Churnet Valley Railway

Cheddleton Station, Cheddleton, Leek, Staffordshire 3 miles (5km) from Leek, off A520 to Stone; ST13 7EE
☎ 01538 360522 Sundays;
www.churnetvalleyrailway.co.uk
Open: Weekends, Bank Holiday Mondays and some weekdays in high season. Ornate Victorian station building housing café, souvenir shop and small relics museum. Also signal box and locomotive display hall.

Places to Visit

Picnic area. Steam rides on most open days. Regular special events.

Foxfield Steam Railway

Blythe Bridge ST11 9BG
☎ 01782 396210
www.foxfieldrailway.co.uk
Open: Apr–Oct Sundays and Bank Holidays, some Saturdays. Museum open on Wed (not Oct) as well. First train 11.30am. Museum, shop, buffet and bar and 5 mile (8 km) steam trips on colliery line to Dilhorne.

Ⓟ ♿ � <15 ☂

Deep Hayes Country Park

2 miles (3.2km) west of Leek, off A53
☎ 01785 277264
www.staffordshire.gov.uk
Mix of woods, meadows and pools with self-guided walks and nature trails. Visitor centre, picnic area, small shop.

Consall Nature Park

Consall
☎ 01543 871773
Open: all year, small shop open Apr– Sep. Walks, fishing and picnic facilities; visitor centre with displays on nature conservation.

Froghall Wharf

A52 Ashbourne to Stoke road
Picnic area and restored limekilns

Canal Boat Trips

From Froghall Wharf ST10 2HJ
☎ 01538 266486
Open: end of May to early Sep
Crew in period costume offer canal trips with Sunday lunch or Sunday afternoon tea. Plus Thursday mornings at 10.30am pre-booking recommended trips and group charter throughout the week.

Froghall Visitor Centre

At Froghall Station on Churnet Valley Railway; ST10 2HA
☎ 01543 871773 for information

Wilboarclough

Hilly Billy Ice Cream Farm

Blaze Farm, off A54 near Allgreave
☎ 01260 227229
Open: daily, all year, 9.30am to dark in winter, 9.30am-6pm in summer
Working hill farm, nature trails, home-made ice cream and tea room.

Rudyard

Rudyard Lake

ST13 8XB 3 miles (5km) north of Leek, A523
Lake Ranger ☎ 01538 306280
www.rudyardlake.com
Shop/café open Easter–end-Sep otherwise weekends, boat launch slipway, bird watching, angling, walking, cycling.

Ⓟ ♿ shop & cafe

Rudyard Lake Steam Railway

3 miles (5km) north of Leek, A523
ST13 8PF
☎ 01538 306704
www.rlsr.org
Open: every Sun and Bank Holiday from late Feb–Oct plus Sat Easter–end-Sept.

Ⓟ ♿ � <12 ☂

Macclesfield

Macclesfield Heritage Centre and Silk Museum

Heritage Centre, Roe Street
☎ 01625 612045
www.macclesfieldsilkmuseum.org
Open: Mon–Sat 11am-5pm, (April – end Oct). Closed Sundays, New Year's Day, Good Friday, Christmas Day and Boxing Day. Admission fee charged.
First museum in Britain to be devoted entirely to the study of the silk industry. Award winning audio-visual programme. Costume, textiles, room settings, scale models. Museum shop. Tea room.

Silk Museum & Paradise Mill

Park Lane SK11 6TJ

☎ 01625 612045

www.silk-macclesfield.org

Open: Mon–Sat. Guided tours of the mill at 12.15pm, 1.30pm, 2.45pm. Closed Sunday (tour takes c.one hour). Admission fee charged. Paradise Mill Heritage Centre/Shop. Demonstrations of weaving. Jacquard handlooms in their original setting. Exhibitions and room settings. Museum shop.

๓ kids free ☎

West Park Museum

Prestbury Road

☎ 01625 612045

Open: Tue-Sun 1.30-4.30pm, (1-4pm from Nov–Mar), closed Mon, 1 Jan, Good Friday, Christmas Day and Boxing Day.

Wide range of fine and decorative art material and objects relating to local history. Also a small but significant collection of Egyptian antiquities. The museum is a venue for a variety of touring exhibitions.

Adlington Hall

Mill Lane, Adlington, SK10 4LF

5 miles (8km) north of Macclesfield, off A523

☎ 01625 827595

www.adlingtonhall.com

Open: 1.30-5pm, Wed only, Jun, Jul and Aug.

Mainly 15th-century manor house, 17th-century organ played by Handel. Landscaped gardens. Tea room

Capesthorne Hall

Siddington, Macclesfield SK11 9JY

☎ 01625 861221

www.capesthorne.com

Open: Apr–Oct inclusive, Sun-Mon and all Bank Holidays. Park, gardens and chapel 12-5pm; hall 1.30-4 pm. Last admission to hall at 3.30pm.

House dated from 1719 with substantial nineteenth-century alterations. Georgian chapel, Mill Wood Walk, gardens with nature trail (suitable for wheelchairs), park and lakes, café and craft shop.

ⓟ ♿ partial to house ๓<16 ☎

Gawsworth Hall

Gawsworth, 2.5 miles (4km) south of Macclesfield just off the A536 SK11 9RN

☎ 01260 223456

www.gawsworthhall.com

Open: May–June, Sun–Wed 2–5pm and special events; July–end of Aug, daily 2–5pm. Striking fifteenth-century half-timbered hall with beautiful gardens. Special events in the open-air theatre with covered grandstand, mid-June to mid-August.

ⓟ ♿ ๓<16 ☎

Disley

Lyme Hall and Park

(National Trust)

Disley, Stockport, SK12 2NR

Disley, 6 miles (9.7km) from Stockport

☎ 01663 762023

www.nationaltrust.org.uk

Open: House mid-March–end-Oct, 11am–5pm Fri–Tue. Gardens mid-March–end-Oct daily, 11am–5pm. Weekends Nov and Dec before Christmas. Park open all year during daylight hours.

1,400 acre (566 ha) with red and fallow deer. 17 acres (6.8 ha) of historic gardens. Hall has many treasures including a large clock collection, Grinling Gibbons' carvings and Mortlake tapestries. Restaurant, coffee shop (in park) and shop.

Background

The infant Dove and Manfold both rise close to the Travellers Rest Inn at Flash Bar some 7.5 miles (12km) up the Buxton road out of Leek. The River Dove forms the county boundary between Derbyshire and Staffordshire. Its source is found in a small well close to the road, marked with intertwined initials of CC and IW – Charles Cotton and Izaak Walton. A replica of the monogram carved on the fishing house in Beresford Dale downstream, this was erected in 1851, two centuries after they famously fished and wrote about the waters of the river. The Manifold's source can also be seen from the road, just to the south of the inn. Starting in a shallow depression, it is deeply cut into the landscape before leaving the field in which it rises.

Geology

The upper reaches of both rivers are spectacular. Take the Hollinsclough road from the Traveller's Rest Inn. The road soon climbs Edge Top where one can pull off the road and view both valleys at the same time. At this point the Manifold has cut deeply into the gritstone formations but the more spectacular view is towards Hollinsclough and the hills beyond. It is here that the overlying grits are replaced by the older

limestones. These are chiefly bedded, but characteristic of this side of the limestone and gritstone boundary are the limestone reef knolls, which have not yet yielded in the same way to the forces of erosion.

The result is a succession of hills on the edge of the limestone plateau, which stretch down the Dove and the Manifold. Examples include Hollins Hill, Chrome Hill, Parkhouse Hill, High Wheeldon, Thorpe Cloud, and Thor's Cliff. These are the closest approximations to 'peaks' in the Peak District.

Beyond Hollinsclough, the character of the two valleys changes. The Dove flows through a deep limestone valley past Crowdecote towards Hartington, while the Manifold, still flowing across the softer overlying shales, occupies a very broad and shallow valley. This difference can easily be seen by taking the Longnor to Sheen road, running along the rounded bluff between the rivers that at one point are less than a mile apart.

Below Hartington and Hulme End, both rivers occupy gorge-like valleys cut deeply into the limestone. The broad valley of the Manifold suddenly ends at the huge limestone dome of Ecton Hill. Hereafter it is characterised by huge incised meanders (a geological term approximating to large loops in a river found in a deep gulley rather than a flat meadowland) until the two rivers unite. It is these meanders ('many folds') that give the river its name, and they create an ever-changing subject for the eye and camera. As a result the scenery is more varied than the Dove Valley until one reaches the Milldale to Thorpe Cloud section of the River Dove.

This is Dovedale – a majestic stretch of the valley now unfortunately suffering from over-use by people. With its natural ash woods, numerous towers of natural stone and features such as Pickering Tor, The Twelve Apostles, Reynard's Arch and the Watchbox near Ilam Rock, it has much to commend it. Dovedale is protected by the National Trust and the dale forms the major part of the Trust's South Peak Estate. It is also a Site of Special Scientific Interest, Grade 1, because of its ancient ash wood. While many people stop at Ilam Rock few glance down river to try and spot the Watchbox, a huge mass of stone perched high on the cliffs of the Derbyshire bank. It is supposed to be capable of being rocked by hand, but the author has never tried to prove whether this is true.

Union of the rivers

Between Ilam and Thorpe the two rivers unite. The Manifold is by far the larger river but, as the Dove is the county boundary, the latter carries its name down-stream from here until it reaches the River Trent near Burton. One of the main tributaries of these two rivers is the Hamps which flows off Morridge near to Leek, in a very broad valley to Waterhouses where it too reaches the limestone and enters a deeply incised valley like the Manifold. It twists and turns with almost

Disappearing rivers

An unusual feature of both the Hamps and the Manifold is the disappearance of the water during dry spells. The Hamps is swallowed up at Waterhouses down solution cavities in the limestone known as 'swallets' or elsewhere in the Peak as 'shack-holes'. There are more swallets at Wetton Mill on the Manifold (on private ground) and a second group can be seen from the road below Wetton Mill at Redhurst, just before the Wetton road begins to climb out of the valley. Both rivers occupy different underground channels and do not appear to unite. Coloured dyes take some 22-24 hours to re-emerge at the boil-holes in the grounds of Ilam Hall, close to the riverside path.

monotonous regularity until it joins the Manifold beneath the huge cliffs of Beeston Tor, which was purchased by the National Trust in 1976.

Human settlement

The deep valleys have had a major influence on the distribution and location of the small villages scattered throughout the area. The upper and less productive soils have resulted in scattered farmhouses rather than communities. Expanding in the 18th century at the junction of two turnpike roads, Longnor is the only village of any size in the moorland area. Elsewhere the villages are situated on the rolling plateau above the valleys, with the notable exceptions of Hartington and Ilam. Waterhouses assumed some importance with the coming of the Manifold Valley Light Railway in 1904 although the railhead at Hulme End failed to develop, primarily because of the economic unimportance of its existence. The only towns of any size outside the area are at Buxton, Leek and Ashbourne, each exerting some influence.

Human settlement can be traced back to the Palaeolithic or Old Stone Age period. Many of the caves in the valleys have yielded evidence of early occupation, chiefly for shelter, although some such as Ossom's Cave at Wetton Mill are known to have been occupied as a workshop for fashioning flints. Even the large Thor's Cave was occupied at one stage. Many of the finds of these caves can be viewed in Buxton Museum, while other finds from Thor's Cave now form part of the Bateman Collection in Sheffield Museum.

Many burials were made in the numerous 'lows' or tumuli which are scattered across the area, chiefly east of the River Manifold. Excavation of these was undertaken by Thomas Bateman, a 19th-century barrow-digger. Victorian antiquarians are usually frowned upon as their techniques were often crude and the results poorly documented. Bateman was somewhat better than most of his contemporaries, although he did open four burial mounds (at Hurdlow, close to the Earl Sterndale to Brierlow Bar road) in one day!

In Dowel Dale near Glutton, is a cave situated close to the road and just above Dowall Hall Farm. Excavation of this cave yielded a communal burial of late Neolithic (or New Stone Age) date. There were skeletons of ten people, ranging from a baby to an old man, interred in the cave. Excavations by the Peakland Archaeological Society at Fox Hole Cave on High Wheeldon have yielded remains dating back to the Middle Stone Age.

The Bronze Age and Iron Age

These are represented in the area through cave and tumuli excavation. There are none of the hill forts in the area that characterise other parts of the Peak. The Bronze Age people used caves for shelter but buried their dead in barrows or mounds of earth, which were raised over a grave or a cremation. A good example of a barrow can be seen adjacent to the road at the Liffs on the Hartington to Alsop road, east of Biggin Dale, just into the field at the top of the hill. Liffs Low contained a cist made of slabs of limestone and contained two sets of flint axes, flint spearheads, flint knives and flint arrowheads amongst much other material.

The more recent history of the area shows little Roman influence, although it was occupied and farmed by Romano-British settlers at the time. However a Roman dish has recently been found at Castern Hall and is now in the British Museum. A motte and bailey castle was established north of Hartington at Pilsbury in Norman times, but little is known about it and full details await excavation. There is, however a useful interpretation board, which enables the layout of this complex site – alongside a public footpath up the valley – to be better appreciated.

The caves of the Manifold have also yielded a further find of much interest. During excavation of St Bertram's Cave at Beeston Tor in 1924, forty-nine Anglo-Saxon silver pennies of about AD871-4 were recovered together with two silver brooches and three gold rings. All are now preserved in the British Museum.

The Middle Ages

In the Middle Ages parts of the area became the property of several different religious orders; for example, a small level platform at Musden Grange near Ilam is the supposed remains of the monastic grange. Following the dissolution of the monasteries, the lands passed into private ownership and thereafter much land was under the influence of families such as the Dukes of Devonshire at Hartington, Ecton and Wetton (the eldest male child of the Duke of Devonshire is in fact titled Lord Hartington). Other estates were those of the Harpur Crewes at Calke Abbey (who owned much land around Warslow, Longnor and Alstonefield) and the FitzHerberts at Tissington.

Famous people

Historical and literary associations with the area are numerous, particularly as a result of the popularity of Dovedale. Byron and Dr Johnson for example were visitors to the dale; Jean Jacques Rousseau knew it during his exile at nearby Wootton Hall; William Morris and other pre-Raphaelites, as well as Mark Twain, were visitors to Sir Thomas Wardle at Swainsley in the Manifold Valley.

Perhaps the greatest name associated with the Dove is that of Izaak Walton who used to stay with his close friend – who became his adopted son – Charles Cotton. Cotton owned the Beresford Hall estate through which flowed the Dove. Beresford Dale was one of the prettiest places on the whole of the river, although Dutch elm disease killed many trees and their removal has marred the dale. It was here that Cotton built a fishing house, dated 1674, which still survives. Cotton added chapters to Walton's *Compleat Angler* in the fifth edition before Walton died, his fame assured. Cotton also owned Throwley Hall (the ruins of which can be seen from the Calton to Ilam road) but both Beresford and Throwley Halls are now no more. Only a Prospect Tower survives at Beresford, which itself had been reduced to ground level before being rebuilt in the 19th century. The fishing house is on private land, but can be seen from the footpath as one approaches the trees at the north end of the dale from Hartington.

Local employment

In the past, people of the area found work chiefly in agriculture and to a lesser extent in the extractive industries or small waterpowered mills. There is not a great deal to see of these former activities although early enclosures around Calton and south-east of Longnor preserve the ancient strip pattern of cultivation in the narrow fields that survive. The insular nature of former village communities seems to be reflected at Butterton where the field walls are built almost as circles around the village. Narrow cultivation terraces – or lynchets – can quite frequently be found in the lower parts of the valleys. A particularly fine set can be seen near Throwley Hall from the opposite side of the valley (ie south of Wetton), particularly when the sun is low in the sky. They are situated in the shallow valley between Throwley and Beeston Tor. The early strip field system is preserved well in the fields to the west of the Buxton-Ashbourne road, between the turnings to Tissington.

Much of the stone for dry stone walls was quarried locally and many small quarries and lime kilns can be found. There are several, for instance, in Hartington Dale between the village and its old railway station. It was quite common for a farmer to have his own lime kiln to burn stone for his land. A good quality gritstone was even mined at Daisy Knoll Farm, Longnor, providing much of the building stone for the village.

There are also many mines in the area. In the millstone grit of Axe Edge coal was mined, while lower downstream lead, copper and zinc ores were extracted which yielded varying fortunes or losses for the miners. At Ecton near Warslow, various mines, which produced considerable quantities of copper ore, can be observed from the roads or footpaths. The main mine reached a total depth of over 1,400ft (451m) – the deepest mine in Britain in the 18th century – and made a considerable fortune for the Duke of Devonshire, its owner. It had

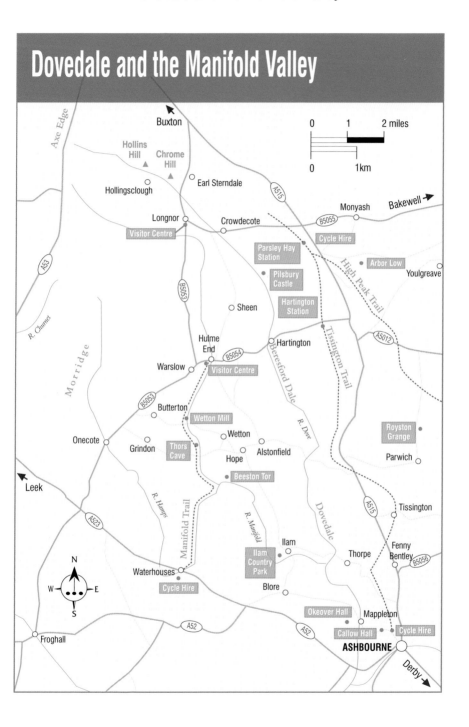

Dovedale and the Manifold Valley

an early example of a Boulton and Watt steam engine, an underground canal for haulage purposes and several other unusual features including an underground waterwheel for pumping.

Recent exploration of some of the oldest workings at Ecton has resulted in the finding of prehistoric hammer stones, and an antler, which may have been used for digging. The latter has been radio carbon dated to 4,000 years old. Your author has also recently found documentary proof that the mines were worked in the 1640s prior to the Civil War. Gunpowder was first used for blasting purposes in this country here at Ecton, around 1670.

The waters of the main streams have long been used for water power. There were medieval mills at Hartington, Ilam and Okeover. The cornmill at Lode Mill near Alstonefield remains intact, while Hartington Mill has been converted into a house. Longnor's sawmill is also slowly being rebuilt as a house. Some of the water mills have had a varied history.

Brund Mill, west of Sheen was built in 1760 as a cornmill, but in 1790 this fine building was converted into a cotton mill by Thomas Cantrell, who fell into financial difficulties four years later. It ended its days grinding corn during World War II and slowly fell into disrepair before being tastefully converted to a dwelling retaining much of the machinery. Thomas Cantrell also had a cotton mill in Hartington, which was built about 1776 on the site of what is now Minton House. The little cottages opposite were probably for his family; they bear the initials T & JC 1777.

Little industry has survived to the present day. One notable exceptions is the silica fire-brick works at Friden, a remnant of long established industries. Cheese was formerly made at Glutton Bridge north of Longnor and Derby cheese was made at Reapsmoor. Both these buildings survive, but the factory established in old mine buildings at Ecton in the 1920s closed in 1933 and all buildings there have been demolished. A further cheese factory existed at Hopedale, near Alstonefield.

The Friden works commenced extracting sand from local pits in 1892. These are unusual pockets found in the limestone and the deposits are still being worked by DSF Refractories Ltd, making bricks for furnace hearth linings.

Despite being so rural, the area was served by three railway lines. The Buxton to Ashbourne line was the most recent, for work commenced as late as 1890. At Parsley Hay it joined the Cromford and High Peak Railway for a while before leaving the latter to enter Buxton. The Cromford and High Peak Railway (discussed later) was built much earlier.

Of more interest perhaps is the narrow gauge (30in (76cm)) railway that ran down the Hamps Valley and up the Manifold Valley from Waterhouses to Hulme End. This railway opened in 1904 and ran for 30 years. The old station buildings (except the coach shed) still remain at Hulme End. It was an unusual railway, with locomotives modelled on those from a narrow gauge line in India.

The River Dove

The **River Dove** rises on Axe Edge, close to the Leek to Buxton Road. Although it is only a small stream, it has a pronounced valley within half a mile (800m) or so of the source. It flows below Brand Top, where the simple war memorial records the loss of five men from one family. There are a lot of pack-horse routes in this area and footpaths now follow these old trails. Several cross the infant river with a single large slab of stone acting as a bridge. A substantial packhorse bridge survives at Washgate, 2 miles (3.2km) below the source. It has low walls to allow uninterrupted passage of the horses and their side panniers.

The river valley widens as Hollinsclough is reached and the river flows below the reef knolls of Hollins Hill, Chrome, Parkhouse and Hitter Hill before passing High Wheeldon. Lying between Earl Sterndale and Crowdecote, High Wheeldon is a large rounded hill with a cave that has yielded Mesolithic (or Middle Stone Age) remains.

The Dove Valley is unusual in that it is possible to walk down the first 20 miles (32km) of its course, all the way to Ashbourne. You need to use the 1:25000 Ordnance Survey White Peak Map and do it in stages, perhaps as circular walks or with a car waiting ahead.

Below Glutton, the small river trickles along in a deep and fairly wide valley. The harder limestone rocks on the east side are higher than the softer gritstones on the west side. It is relatively quiet all the way down the valley to Hartington where the tourists flock daily. The walking is very pleasant too, through pasture and on farm tracks or quiet lanes. There is a pub – the Packhorse – at Crowdecote, where you can relax before continuing on towards Pilsbury and Hartington.

At **Pilsbury**, there is a motte and bailey castle with an interpretation board, explaining a little about this Norman fortification. Look out for Broadmeadow Hall on the west or Staffordshire side of the valley. It is seventeenth-century and was on the Peak Park's endangered buildings list until its use changed from a barn back to a rather fine looking dwelling. Pilsbury was on an important saltway that crossed the Peak from Cheshire via the Roaches, Mermaid Inn and Brund (where it divided, one route going to Hartington and Wirksworth, the other via Pilsbury to Monyash and on to the eastern side of the Peak).

Hartington is situated where Hartington Dale joins the Dove. The River Hardin which runs down Hartington Dale has a subterranean course and is culverted under Hartington's Market Place. There is a pottery producing terracotta ware and the Hart in the Country shop selling quality items. Hartington also has various tea rooms and The Charles Cotton Hotel (recently refurbished).

The church has some remnants of early decorated plasterwork and the Hall, built in 1611, is claimed to be the best surviving example of a Derbyshire yeoman's house. It was the home of the Bateman family. The other wings were added in 1861 while the farm buildings were built in 1859. The west bays were added in 1911 on the house's 300th anniversary. It is now a youth hostel

continued on p.45

Railway Trails and Cycle Hire

The Peak District has a number of disused railway tracks that have been converted to cycling and walking trails.

These trails are ideal for easy and safe cycling, with cycle hire from many places (see the Fact File for details). Hire is now so popular that it pays to arrive early, or book in advance, especially in the summer and during school holidays. Apart from a short section of the Manifold Valley Trail there is no motor traffic, although care must be taken to avoid walkers.

Middleton Top Engine House

With a little basic map reading it is possible to combine the trails with country lanes, thus making a circular excursion. This is particularly so with the Tissington and High Peak Trails, which meet at Parsley Hay. It is possible to gain access to the trail at most road crossings, although a scramble up the embankment may be necessary.

Remember that the trails do go uphill, even if with only a slight gradient, especially on the Tissington Trail north of Ashbourne and on the inclines of the High Peak Trail. The area around Biggin is the highest point.

The Cromford and High Peak Railway was built like a canal, with long flat sections and inclines between the different levels, so this trail is comparatively level. Both the High Peak and Tissington Trails have reasonable cycling surfaces now (much to the relief of early users of the latter), while the Manifold Valley Trail is surfaced with tarmac.

Manifold Valley Trail

The Manifold Valley Trail commences at Waterhouses where the narrow gauge train used to meet the standard gauge line from Leek. Road widening has caused the loss of some of the station, but the goods shed remains and is now the cycle hire centre. There is ample car-parking which you reach off the road behind the Crown Inn. Go under the old and huge railway bridge and turn left.

The Hamps Valley is very picturesque and is equally enjoyable, whether on foot or on a bike. The latter is a useful means of travelling up the valley to Hulme End, a distance of eight miles. The first station was at Sparrowlea, where there is a tearoom in the adjacent farmhouse.

After four miles (6.5km) is Beeston Tor, where the valley reaches the Manifold Valley. The river bed in both valleys is normally dry in the summer. Beeston Tor is the large cliff of reef limestone opposite the farm. It was here that Saxon coins and jewellery were found during an archaeological dig in 1924. The finds are now in the British Museum.

The trail continues past Weag's Bridge and Thor's Cave to Redhurst, where the old line is shared with vehicles to Swainsley. There is a tea room at Wetton Mill near to the swallet holes where the river dives underground. Some of these may be seen from the road at Redhurst.

Swainsley Tunnel is now lit for safety and here the railway line runs on to Hulme End without vehicular traffic (except for access to land). This trail is flat and tarmaced. You can park at Hulme End, Swainsley, Wetton Mill, Weag's Bridge and Waterhouses. The old booking office and engine shed remain at Hulme End and the former has recently been restored and opened as the Manifold Valley Visitor Centre. Among other displays is a scale model of the Leek and Manifold Valley Light Railway as it ran from Hulme End to Swainsley Tunnel. The Manifold Inn in the hamlet used to be known as the Light Railway Hotel. It serves food and makes a useful place to relax before returning down the valley. It also offers accommodation.

Tissington Trail

The Tissington Trail runs north of Ashbourne. Cycles may be hired north of the railway tunnel, on the road to Mapleton. There is a car park here. It is a climb uphill north of here onto the limestone plateau, but thereafter, it is much easier! There are car parks at Tissington, Alsop-en-le-Dale, Hartington and Parsley Hay. Hartington Station lies 1.5 miles (2.4km) from the village. The trail has good views across the southern Peak District and ends north of Hurdlow Station. Here the line is still in use by the neighbouring limestone quarries. The line north of Parsley Hay was part of the Cromford and High Peak Railway and the trail continues as the High Peak Trail north of Parsley Hay. This latter trail ran down to the Derwent Valley and High Peak Junction. Bikes may be hired at Parsley Hay.

Former Hartington signal box

Railway Trails And Cycle Hire Continued...

South of Parsley Hay, parts of both trails are now nature reserves. On the High Peak Trail, either side of the A515 are large beds of heather. Limestone heathland is now quite rare and most of the areas in which it occurs are protected. Look at the plaques on the bridge carrying the A515. One is dated 1825, which makes this one of the oldest lines in the country.

High Peak Trail

The High Peak Trail is very flat, other than the inclines. It passes Friden Brickworks before reaching the A5012 near Pikehall. At Gotham, the line nearly turns through a right angle in a 55yd (51m) radius, an amazing feature which meant large locomotives could not be used on the line. There are parking and picnic tables at Friden Station as well as Minninglow, near to Gotham Curve.

Beyond Minninglow, look out for several large stonefaced embankments built to keep the line flat. Below Minninglow itself (the site of a chambered tomb) is an old quarry served by the line. The trail winds its way through Longcliffe and more quarries to the Hopton Incline. Originally worked by a stationary haulage engine, this incline was sufficiently shallow for later locomotives to climb it unassisted (the gradient was 1:14). It was the steepest unassisted incline on British Railways. Having levelled out once more, the line runs on to Middleton Top Engine House, where the original steam beam engine survives and is occasionally steamed. Bikes may be hired here.

From Middleton Top, the line descends steeply down Middleton and Sheep Pasture Inclines to the Derwent Valley where there are more relics of the railway, plus the Cromford Canal and picnic tables. The old railway workshops at High Peak Wharf have been preserved and are worth a visit, as is the neighbouring Lea Wood Pumping Engine, especially when it is in steam.

Monsal Trail

The Monsal Trail runs between Blackwell Mill Junction (near Topley Pike and 3 miles (4.8km) east of Buxton) and Coombes viaduct, one mile (1.6km) south-east of Bakewell. Four tunnels have been closed on the grounds of safety and it is necessary to follow a diversion, which is clearly marked. The old railway line was cut high on the valleyside above the River Wye and is now a pleasant walk with memorable views. There are car parks at the former stations at Bakewell and Millers Dale and also near Topley Pike.

The Bakewell to Longstone section is suitable for cyclists and horse riders. For the disabled, there are level surfaces in either direction from Bakewell and Millers Dale stations.

Sett Valley Trail

The Sett Valley Trail runs to New Mills from Hayfield Station site. Car-parking is available and there is a heritage trail at the New Mills end.

offering private rooms, some ensuite, as well as more traditional dormitory accommodation. You can call in for a drink at the bar or an evening meal in the restaurant even if you are not staying there.

The village is one of the major tourist centres of the Peak. The attractiveness of the village lies in the architectural variety of the houses around the square. It is a sobering thought that such in-dividuality of design and construction, all of houses built before planning constraints, seems to be so frowned upon by the planners today, although quite rightly they insist on buildings being built in the local stone. It is a good starting point for walks in the area, particularly into Dovedale.

The former Hartington railway station is now a picnic site with toilet facilities, while the railway track has been converted into the **Tissington Trail**. There is an **information centre in the old signal box,** which still retains its original lever frames, and several photographs on the wall show what the railway used to look like. The trail gives level walking and cycling north from Ashbourne. Cycles may be hired from the National Park at Parsley Hay Wharf (SK147636) and Ashbourne (SK175470). If you hire a cycle from Parsley Hay and end up in Hartington, it is better to return via Long Dale, as it is a much easier gradient. Proceed eastwards out of the village, past the school and take the first turn to the left, into Long Dale. Sections of this valley are part of the **Derbyshire Dales National Nature Reserve.**

Below Hartington, the valley becomes a gorge, the meadows ending abruptly at **Beresford Dale**. Charles Cotton lived in Beresford Hall, but it had become a ruin by 1850 and has now gone completely. The dale used to be quite dark from the leaf cover, but Dutch elm disease completely changed the dale's character. Look out for the **Prospect Tower** rebuilt in 1905-6 with stone from the remains of the hall, and also for the **fishing temple**. The latter is situated on a bend in the river and dates from 1674.

The valley is deeper in the next dale, **Wolfscote Dale**, and the character stays like this all the way to beyond Milldale, where it becomes more wooded. **Milldale** is a popular place, despite being very small. It has a small shop that also sells refreshments, car park and toilets. The valley path uses the road between Lode Mill (a lead smelter built in 1760) and Milldale. However a path runs along the top of the valley from Milldale to the Lode Mill to Alsop-en-le-Dale road with splendid views down into the dale. The National Trust rightly has resisted pressure to open the other side of the river to ramblers – it is the last piece of limestone pasture in the valley on the Derbyshire side to remain without a path. Here is a good case of conserva-tion taking priority over visitors.

Below Milldale lies **Dovedale,** with its limestone tors and relict ash wood, now a Grade 1 Site of Special Scientific Interest. The valley is very popular, and a causeway built along the pathway seems to contain the pressure from over a million visitors each year. The area around the tall **Ilam Rock** is particularly scenic. There is a footbridge here and land on which to sit and

Tissington Hall

*The former railway track,
Manifold Valley*

*Manifold Valley Visitor Centre,
Hulme End Station*

Opposite page: Ilam Rock, Dovedale

absorb the beauty around you. There used to be a wooden tearoom at the west end of the footbridge but this has long gone. The bridge takes one over to the path in Hall Dale and affords an opportunity to watch the fish and wild ducks on the river. The freestanding tors in Dovedale are probably the tallest in the Peak District.

Below Ilam Rock are **Pickering Tors**, the **Lion Head Rock**, **Tissington Spires** and **Lovers Leap** before one reaches the **Stepping Stones** and the end of the gorge. The valley then becomes much more shallow as it continues on to Coldwall Bridge – a huge and unused turnpike era road bridge – Mapleton and the Okeover estate.

The section between Beresford Dale and the Stepping Stones differs from the rest of the valley. The river is flowing across a gravelly limestone river bed, the water is crystal clear and the path tends to hug the river. It therefore creates more interest than walking through the middle of river meadows, which characterise the rest of the Dove and the Manifold/Hamps light railway trail.

At the Stepping Stones you can leave the Dove and climb up Lin Dale to reach **Thorpe** and the Peveril of the Peak Hotel, which is built at the side of the footpath. When most visitors came by train (or on foot) from Ashbourne, this was the main way to Dovedale. Beyond the Stepping Stones, the river joins the Manifold below the Izaak Walton Hotel. The dining room here looks out onto Dovedale and has one of the best views from any hotel dining room in the country.

The River Hamps

West of Dovedale lie the Manifold Valley and the upper basin of the **River Hamps**. Paths across the area are recommended to ramblers and it is easy to organise a circular route. There are many paths in this valley all the way down to Winkhill on the A523, where the valley becomes flat and featureless before turning north and into the limestone. At **Mixon** there are the remains of an old copper mine, which was last worked in 1858. North of the mine are two nineteenth-century dams, although they no longer impound water. They remain as relics of the old mine. Spring is a good time of year for walking here. Marsh marigolds and lady's smock add a splash of colour to the lush vegetation as one strolls along in quiet and unspoilt surroundings. Downstream there is little of interest in Onecote village, but the small collection of houses in **Ford** 1.5 miles (2.4km) further downstream is often missed by visitors and is a very tranquil spot.

The River Hamps changes its character completely at **Waterhouses**, where it leaves the grit and shales and enters limestone country. The river often disappears underground for months on end in dry weather, but rises again at Ilam. The valley meanders between steep hillsides to **Beeston Tor**, where it meets the Manifold Valley.

The track bed of the old light railway runs up the valley from Waterhouses. Cyclists are now permitted on the track and there are cycle-hire facilities in the old station car park and at Brown End Farm in Waterhouses. It presents a marvellous way of exploring the Manifold

Valley as far as Hulme End. The best way to return is down the same track; there is as much of interest travelling back as one sees when travelling up the valley, although the exposed limestone cliffs and caves are a feature not of the Hamps but of the Manifold Valley.

River Manifold

The **River Manifold** like its neighbour, the River Dove, rises on Axe Edge and flows off the gritstone moors. Both run close together in deeply incised valleys as far as Longnor. The main packhorse route between Flash and Longnor is now tarmac covered and runs along the aptly named Edge Top, giving marvellous views down into the deep valley that carries the infant waters of the Manifold towards Longnor. Beyond the valley is the moor of Middle Hills and **Flash** village, the highest village in England.

Longnor is a compact village built of local stone mined at Daisy Knoll, on the Hollinsclough road. Even the bricks of the former Crewe and Harpur Arms were made locally, at Reapsmoor, 3 miles (2.4km) to the south. Longnor is not at all pretentious, but it is none the worse for that. A recent development has been the small industrial estate near the fire station where clock manufacture is an unusual industry, but one not unknown to the region. Another surprising development on this site is **Upper Limits**, an indoor climbing wall, available to individuals proficient in rock climbing skills. For beginners and improvers there are courses or individual tuition. There are also facilities for archery here.

The village is a useful centre for exploring the upper reaches of the Manifold and Dove valleys. It has three pubs serving food, together with a very pleasant **Craft Centre** in the Market Hall, dated 1873, which retains its toll board for buyers and sellers at nineteenth-century Longnor markets and fairs. Cakes and snacks are available, including 'oaties'. Made in nearby Warslow, these have a variety of fillings in a traditional north Staffordshire oatcake. They are well worth a try! The centre has permanent displays of paintings by local artists, which are for sale.

Below Longnor the valley widens out into flat riverside meadows that are used for haymaking. Although it is not possible to walk down the valley to Longnor, below the village, paths and minor roads can be taken to walk to **Hulme End**.

Ahead lies the rounded form of **Ecton Hill**, heralding the start of the limestone and the more attractive section of the valley. At Ecton are the remains of the old copper mine. Today, the mines are quiet and the shafts flooded. Above river level, a generation of mining-industry students have used the hillside and its workings for practical fieldwork. Discerning ramblers use the paths over the hill, the extensive views stretching far away in all directions.

Sitting high on the hillside above the old mine tips, the numerous yellow flowers of the mountain pansy, which prefer a slightly acidic soil, wave about in the breeze. Below, the line of the old narrow-gauge railway threads down the valley and ruined mine buildings and stone tips may be clearly seen.

Two hundred years ago the scene

49

Well Dressing

Many Derbyshire villages owe their location to a reliable flow of pure water. Springs are especially important on the limestone plateau, where water quickly seeps into cracks in the rock. A regular flow was of particular importance during periods of drought or pestilence such as the Black Death. The plague was prevalent in the area from medieval times to the seventeenth century, the village of Curbar being a victim in 1632 and Eyam in 1665-6. Tissington's wells are reputed to have maintained their purity during an outbreak of plague in 1348-9.

Thus the custom of 'dressing' or adorning village wells with flowers may have originated as thanks for the supply of pure water. The custom has been practised for over 300 years, as a visitor to Staffordshire in 1680 noted that 'They have also a custom in this county … of adorning their wells with boughs and flowers' and that the custom was associated with 'cakes, ale and a little music and dancing.'

Today the wells are decorated with flower petals pressed into clay held in a wooden framework. It is a difficult task that combines hard work with artistic skill. The clay must be cleaned of impurities before being made into the consistency of plaster. The frames must be soaked (perhaps in the village pond, as at Tissington) to prevent the clay from drying out. The trays often have rows of protruding nails to prevent the damp clay from falling away when the frames are vertical.

The design is sketched onto the wet clay, and then flower petals, berries, moss, lichen, seeds and cones are pressed into the surface. The collecting of the flowers and their application must all be done at the last minute to keep the display looking as fresh as possible. The time of year will determine the types of colour available; wells that are decorated early such as at Tissington can have problems with the availability of certain flowers, especially if spring comes late.

The custom is now carried on in many villages in and around the Peak District throughout the spring and summer. With its five wells, Tissington is the best known; Barlow (north-west of Chesterfield) claims to have dressed wells for the longest unbroken period; while Hartington is one of the most recent to start the tradition. A full list of villages which dress their wells is given in the Fact File.

Left: Hall Well, Tissington

Cottages, Hartington

Longnor

was quite different. At the bend in the road stood a smelting house and to the north of the little cabin existed another smelter. To the north of that stood a brick calcining kiln, built like a bottle oven in the Potteries. Between here and the roadside cottage with its lime trees (the old mine manager's house) stood another roadside cottage and the mine school where seventy children learnt their three Rs. On the far south of the site, where the flat, stony ground exists by the roadside, was another smelter with a waterwheel. On the side of the hill were several other buildings and the main entrance for bringing out the ore was in the garden of the house with the distinctive green spire. To the right of the hill, Beresford Hall would probably have been visible.

Five hundred years earlier, the area was a deer park that stretched south-wards from Apes Tor. The stone wall that runs along the hillside, high above the valley bottom, marked its east side and the river probably marked its west side. To the north, a windmill would have been visible at Sheen and Hart-ington Mill probably existed, and it is probable that some of the mine work-ings were extant.

Mining took place in the area, for there is a charming record noting the prosecution of the vicar of Blore in 1376 for stealing lead ore valued at £10 at Grindon. In the fields around the Manifold, the myriad stone walls seen today would not have existed and there was probably much more woodland. Across the valley at Warslow, the old field system of strips would have been visible with the characteristic ridge and furrows that still survive.

RAF memorial

Grindon Church has a monument to a Royal Air Force crew who died when their plane, bringing food, crashed on Grindon Moor in the harsh winter of 1946-47. It was heading for a large cross in the fields near to Butterton which marked the drop zone. Curiously this was the fifth Royal Air Force plane to come down near Butterton, as four crashes had occurred on or near Butterton Moor in 1935-36.

Today, many visitors wend their way to **Wetton Mill** and on to Thor's Cave, past limestone crags and the water swal-lets that take all the river water except in winter and periods of heavy rain. **Thor's Cave** rises 350 ft (107m) high above the river, its 60ft (18m) entrance a disappointing promise of a good cave system beyond.

I once spent a July evening in the valley with Frank Oulsnam, then the National Trust's warden for this area. He probably knows more of the val-ley's flora and fauna than anyone. We started at Apes Tor, at Ecton, which is owned by the Trust. The scent of flowers was most striking – it always seems to be strongest around here. Common spotted and fragrant orchids were in flower as well as the butterfly orchid. The smell of aniseed emanated from beds of sweet cicely; north-facing habitats were lush with beds of rose-bay willow herb, meadow-sweet and the ox-eye daisy.

Down on the river, the water was low and a moorhen strutted about on smooth stones, ignoring us completely. On the mine tips, thyme was in flower, mercifully safe from flower pickers behind a new stout fence. Eventually, we reached **Weag's Bridge**, where the ancient pack horse road from Grindon to Alstonefield crosses the river. We traded detail on habitats and history as night drew in and it started to rain. We speculated on whether the fire-flies still dance in the night air and I quietly reflected that, for me, this valley is one of the best in the whole of England.

Beyond Weag's Bridge is Beeston Tor, where the Manifold meets the Hamps. From here there is no path down the valley floor. A lane climbs from Ilam to Throwley, where the old hall remains have been stabilised and a path from Wetton to Castern cuts across the valley rim above the nature reserve. Both give glimpses into what must be the prettiest dale in the Peak without access to the public – and long may it remain so.

Beyond is Ilam country park owned by the National Trust, but best visited on the quiet days during the week rather than in the bustle of weekends and Bank Holidays. Below Ilam, the valley loses its name to the Dove which has been, and continues to be, the county boundary, despite being the minor of the two rivers. The Dove flows down to Hanging Bridge on the outskirts of Ashbourne, which describes itself as 'The Gateway to Dovedale'.

Ashbourne

Ashbourne is the main town serving the area. Primarily a market town, it retains many eighteenth-century buildings together with other much older buildings in its main streets such as the Gingerbread Shop, which is timber framed and thought to be fifteenth-century. The Lamplight Restaurant in the Butchery is of a similar age. It is probable that the town was originally situated further to the west and nearer the church, which is now almost out of the town, but development of a new centre, including the market place, probably began as early as the thirteenth century.

Places to look out for in the town include the **Green Man and Black's Head Royal Hotel**. Its inn sign stretches over the street, and it has a small courtyard where coaches unloaded. Look at the Black's Head carved on the gallows-style inn sign; on one side he smiles, on the other he is sad. Of Georgian origin, the inn has associations with Boswell, who along with Dr Johnson stayed in the town with Dr Taylor who owned the Mansion in Church Street. Unfortunately, the 'Black's Head' in the name has recently been dropped. The Mansion House is of seventeenth-century origin with a brick façade, and a porch similar to the Grey House opposite, dating from the mid-eighteenth century. Next door to the Mansion is the Old House, also built in the eighteenth century.

A walk along the street towards the church is very rewarding. There are many Georgian houses of interest including No 61, the Grey House, which is next to the Old Grammar School. Sir Nikolaus Pevsner described Church Street as one of the finest streets in Derbyshire. The Grammar School was founded in 1585. The central portion

The Winster Morris Dancers at Hartington

Compton, Ashbourne

St Johns Street, Ashbourne

Church Street, Ashbourne

Shrovetide Football Ashbourne: Playing in the street (above) Balls hanging in the Ashbourne Ex-Working Men's Club, Market Place

with four gables above was the old schoolroom and the school-master's accommodation was at either side, while opposite are the almshouses built in 1614-30.

While in the street, visit **St Oswald's Church**, one of the grandest in the Peak, preferably in early spring when the churchyard is submerged beneath a carpet of daffodils. The oldest part of the existing building dates from the thirteenth century upon an earlier site, from which a Norman crypt has been located. The chancel was dedicated on the 24 April 1241, the date being recorded by the oldest known inscribed brass plate in the country. Most of the building dates from the fourteenth century. The spire rises to a height of 212 ft (65m).

The alabaster monuments in the church are especially notable, as well as a fine carving in marble of Penelope Boothby. The daughter of the owners of Ashbourne Hall was painted by Reynolds (this painting inspired the famous 'Bubbles' advert of Pear's Soap). The carving is by Banks and was exhibited at the Royal Academy. Penelope's death caused the breakup of her parent's marriage and the pitiful story became well known. It was quite common for little girls to attend fancy dress parties dressed as 'Penelope'. A guide book about the church is available.

Ashbourne is famed for its **Shrovetide football match**, which occurs on Shrove Tuesday and Ash Wednesday. The ball is thrown up at 2pm in Shaw Croft car park behind the Green Man Inn and the game can continue until 10pm. The highly decorated ball is made of leather filled with cork. The goals are 3 miles (4.75km) apart on the sites of the old Clifton and Sturston Mills and teams, consisting of hundreds, are known as the 'Up'ards' and 'Down'ards'. The rules are few and the town's shops are boarded up for safety; even the river is part of the game. It is the object of each team to get the ball back to its own goal. It is a slow-moving game and rarely are more than two goals scored in a day's play. Ashbourne's game is the last Shrovetide mass football game to be played through the streets of mainland Britain. It has survived several attempts in the nineteenth century to close it down.

The game was also played in Derby, where it was stopped in 1846. This is the origin of the expression 'a Derby game', when two local teams play each other. It is quite a local honour to turn up, or start, the game or to goal the ball. The goaler keeps the ball or, in the event of no goal, it is given to the turner-up.

Ashbourne was also the home of Catherine Booth, the wife of General Booth, the founder of the Salvation Army. There is a plaque to her on a house in Sturston Road, and a bust of her in the park. The town is also famous for its gingerbread and has a growing reputation for its high class clothiers. A recent product of the town was Ashbourne Water, which was pumped from the well at the former Nestlé factory site. A remarkable marketing triumph, it has now gone, like the factory.

There is a swimming pool on the site of the old railway station. Picnic tables are located close to the river in two locations, on Bank Croft behind Lloyds Bank off King Edward Street, and in Fish Pond Meadow in what used to be the grounds of the hall.

Lloyds Bank stands in Compton. The street is particularly wide at this point. This is because the town's unofficial market used to be held here in competition to the chartered market held in Ashbourne, north of the river. Compton despite its proximity to the old town was formerly in the separate parish of Clifton and Compton.

Before moving on from Ashbourne, it is worth mentioning the village of **Norbury**, off the A515 road to Lichfield. About 5 miles (8km) down the Dove Valley from Ashbourne, it has a lovely church, which dates from the early fourteenth century. There is some armorial glass too, dating according to Pevsner from 1300-1307. The rear of the adjacent manor house dates from circa 1250 and was enlarged in 1305. It has been owned by the National Trust since 1987 and is open only by appointment.

Although few of the villages in the area have individual buildings of outstanding architectural merit, many are worth visiting. They are all villages that have enjoyed the patronage of some particular family. What does make them of interest is the variations of vernacular architecture, reflecting changing tastes and different building stones.

North of Ashbourne

Well worth visiting are Fenny Bentley, Tissington and Alstonefield, all accessed from the A515 Ashbourne to Buxton Road. **Fenny Bentley** lies a little way up the A515 Buxton road from Ashbourne. In the church is a curious tomb to Thomas Beresford who fought at Agincourt. The effigies of both Thomas

and his wife are depicted bundled up in shrouds, as are their 21 children around the sides of the tomb. The tower of their fortified and moated manor house may be seen from the A515.

From Fenny Bentley the A515 **Tissington** can be taken to the right through a set of stone gate posts. Beyond is an avenue of lime trees, originally planted in 1815, presumably to commemorate the Battle of Waterloo. They were replaced at the end of the nineteenth century after a number blew down in a storm in 1894. The present avenue was planted in 1970.

Tissington village is worth a visit at any time. **Tissington Hall**, a large and very fine Jacobean mansion, is open to the public in the summer months and a very pleasant tea room has been opened in the old coach house. It is a popular subject for photographers, along with the wells and village pond, while the old railway station site is an access point for the Tissington Trail. Gardeners will enjoy **Tissington Nursery,** which specialises in choice and unusual plants.

A visit to the village on, or just after, Ascension Day to see the annual well dressing ceremony should not be missed. Although well dressing now takes place in many Peakland villages throughout the summer, the ceremony at Tissington is the most well known. At Tissington, five wells (plus a children's well) are 'dressed' to depict varying religious themes. The tradition is supposed to have originated as a thanksgiving for the ceaseless supply of pure water to the village.

North-west of Tissington is **Alstonfield**, with a turning off the A515 opposite the New Inns Hotel (now Holiday Fellowship owned). The village is situated on the limestone plateau, with many solid buildings closely knit together. The church contains seventeenth-century pews, a double-decker pulpit and a chest about 10ft (3m) long probably 700 years old. Part of the building is Norman. A guide book is available in the church (and also at Hartington Church).

In the village there used to be a shop and café plus the gallery of Jean Goodwin, a good local artist painting chiefly in watercolours. There was also a craft shop in the village selling wickerwork, books and gifts situated on the road to Hulme End. Regrettably all has now gone; a common freature in our local villages.

From Alstonfield the road to Wetton descends down to Hope Dale. On the right is the Hope House Costume Museum and Restoration Workshop, which opened in June 1997. Run by Notty Hornblower, the museum centres around Notty's extensive collection of some 300 costumes and 500 accessories. Although by appointment only, visitors can see clothes being restored in the workshop together with a display of costumes and accessories covering the period between 1840 and the 1970s.

Ilam village was rebuilt away from the Gothic Revival style hall in the early years of the nineteenth century. The hall was built for Mr Jesse Watts-Russell between 1821 and 1826, to the design of John Shaw, as a spectacular mansion with towers and turrets. This was during the era when Alton Towers was being built in Tudor Gothic style under the influence of Pugin. The author consid-

ers that Ilam, built in the same style, was an attempt to 'keep up with the Jones's' – or in this case the Earl of Shrewsbury. Snelston Hall, south of Ashbourne, was similar. All three properties were far too large for domestic comfort, but typical of Victorian affluence. The formal buildings of Ilam Hall were demolished in 1935 and the remaining portion is now a youth hostel.

Ilam Hall, the church and the village school are all of interest. There is a National Trust shop, information centre and tea room in the stable block of the Watts-Russell house. The view from the terrace is magnificent and it is easy to see why Ilam Hall was built on this particular site. There are two Saxon crosses in the churchyard and inside the church is the tomb of St Bertram and Sir Francis Chantrey's statue of David Pike-Watts dated 1826. Notice the former Saxon doorway to the right of the porch. The former is very fine indeed and shows Jesse Watts-Russell's father-in-law on his death bed with his daughter and grandchildren at his bedside. The cross in the village near the bridge is dedicated to the daughter, Watts-Russell's wife, Mary.

Also worth exploring are the paths in the wood in the grounds of the hall. One leads to a grotto where William Congreve wrote the Old Bachelor – his stone desk and seat are still there. The path along the valley bottom known as Paradise Walk takes one past the resurging waters of the Manifold and Hamps. Further on it passes the 'Battle Cross' found when the village was remodelled.

The riverside walk takes you past the 'boil holes'. The first and larger one is

Dovedale from Stoney Low, south of Biggin Dale

Wetton, opposite The Ye Olde Yew Tree Inn, now a popular venue for walkers

where the River Manifold can be seen rising after its underground journey from Wetton Mill. The second and smaller boil hole contains the waters of the River Hamps. Other boil holes exist nearby where other water courses return to the surface.

Cave divers have explored the Manifold system for quite a distance. It goes directly under the hall and has been traced into the fields beyond the lane to Castern. This is, of course, quite a dangerous sport, which should be left to the experts. The path continues on to the Riverside Lodge, where you join the Ilam to Castern Road. The last section is private and sometimes a small toll is levied.

In the grounds of the hall, St Bertram's Bridge gracefully spans the river. This was the old road into the village until the houses were moved away from the hall and church.

Places to Visit

℗ Parking Available
& Disabled Facilities
ﭩ Family Attraction
<№ Concession for under certain ages
☂ Suitable in Wet Weather

Hulme End

Manifold Valley Visitor Centre

Old Station buildings
☎ 01298 84679
Open: weekends throughout the year, school holidays and most days in the summer.
Information centre, exhibition on the history of the valley, picnic site.

Hartington

The Old Cheese Shop

Market Place SK17 OAL
☎ 01298 84935
Open: daily, 9am–5pm including Bank Holidays.
℗ & free ☂

Rookes Pottery

Mill Lane, Hartington SK17 OAL
☎ 01298 84650
www.rookespottery.co.uk
Open: weekdays 9.30am–4.30pm, Sat and Sun 10am–4pm. Closed in Jan and Feb.
Terracotta garden pottery made on the premises. Visitors may look round the workshop and see pots in production.
℗ & free entry ☂

High Peak Trail

Middleton Top Engine House

Middleton-via-Wirksworth, Matlock DE4 4LS Signposted off the B5036 Cromford to Wirksworth road
☎ 01629 823204
wwwderbyshire.gov.uk/countryside
℗ & ﭩ<16 ☂

Open: Easter to Oct, 10.30am–5pm. Engine working on 1st weekend in each month and Bank Holiday Sundays and Mondays. Restored beam engines built in 1829 to haul waggons up a 1:8.75 incline on the Cromford and High Peak railway.

Longnor

Upper Limits

Unit 1, Buxton Road SK17 ONZ
☎ 01298 83149
Fax 01298 83857
www.leek.ac.uk/upper-limits
Open: Daily 10am–5pm, Mon–Fri;
10am–4pm, Sat–Sun. Mon, Wed
and Fri evenings, 6–9.30pm. Indoor
climbing wall, climbing, caving and
archery courses.
℗ ⋔ ⌒

Longnor Craft Centre

The Market Hall, Market Square,
SK17 0NT
☎ 01298 83587
Open: Mid-Feb to Christmas Eve daily
10am–5pm; Jan–mid-Feb, Fri–Sun
only.
Exhibits and sale of work by local
craftspeople and artists, including
traditional furniture. Coffee shop.

Tissington

Tissington Hall

DE6 1RA
☎ 01335 352200
Tea room ☎ 01335 350501
www.tissington-hall.com
Open: Phone or check website for
opendays or to arrange a group tour.
Fine Jacobean Manor House. Coach
House tea room adjacent, open
10.30am–5pm, Mar–Oct, daily. Rest of
year Thurs–Sun.
℗ ♿part ⋔concessions ⌒

Tissington Nursery

☎ 01335 390650
www.tissingtonnursery.co.uk
Open: 1 Mar–30 Sep 10am–5pm

On a Wick and a Prayer

Tissington DE6 1RA
☎ 01335 390639
www.onawick.co.uk
Open: Apr–Sep Wed–Fri 10am–4pm,
Sat & Sun 1–5pm. May be open other
times, so ring!

Alstonfield

Hope House Costume Museum and Restoration Workshop

DE6 2GE
☎ 01335 310318
By appointment only for groups. Over
600 items of fashionable dress dress
from late 18th century to 1970s.

Ilam

Ilam Country Park (National Trust)

South Peak Estate Office,Home
Farm, Ilam,Derbyshire, DE6 2AZ
☎ 01335 350503
Shop open: daily Apr–Oct 11am–
5pm. Other weekends 11am–4pm
(excluding Christmas and New Year)
Tearoom: mid-May–mid-Oct, Fri–
Tue 11am–5pm, winter weekends
11am–4pm. Apr–mid-May weekends
11am–5pm.
Five miles (8km) north west of
Ashbourne. Comprises 84 acres of
parkland on the banks of the River
Manifold.

3. The Southern Limestone Plateau

Much of the limestone ditrict of the Peak lies south of Buxton, bounded to the east by the River Derwent. East of Buxton, the River Wye dissects the limestone as it flows to join the Derwent. The district bounded by these valleys is a flattish plateau with interlocking stone walls forming a grey patchwork on a green quilt, dissected by a number of picturesque dales. Occasionally the relief is augmented by clumps of trees or sometimes long lines of trees growing along the old lead mine veins and providing shelter from the penetrating winter wind.

Dotted over the landscape are countless farms, some in small clusters and, less frequently, some grouped together in villages. It is almost a pattern for the district to see the ribbon development of the last two and a half centuries now welded into neat little villages. A good example of the linear pattern can be seen at Youlgreave and is met again in Sheldon, Chelmorton, Taddington, Elton, Bonsall, Winster and Wensley among others.

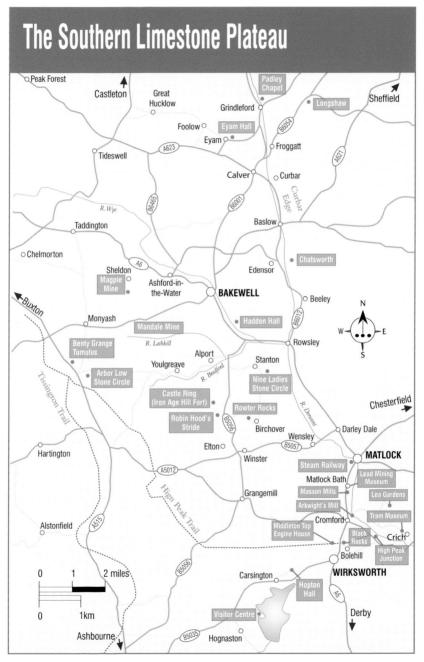

The Southern Limestone Plateau

Peak Forest

Castleton

Great Hucklow

Padley Chapel

Grindleford

Longshaw

Sheffield

B6054

Foolow

Eyam Hall

Eyam

Froggatt

A623

Tideswell

Calver

Curbar

A621

B6465

B6001

Curbar Edge

R. Wye

Baslow

Taddington

Chelmorton

A6

Chatsworth

Sheldon

Edensor

Magpie Mine

Ashford-in-the-Water

BAKEWELL

Beeley

Buxton

Monyash

Mandale Mine

Haddon Hall

B6012

Benty Grange Tumulus

R. Lathkill

Alport

Rowsley

Arbor Low Stone Circle

Youlgreave

Stanton

R. Bradford

Nine Ladies Stone Circle

Chesterfield

Tissington Trail

Castle Ring (Iron Age Hill Fort)

Rowter Rocks

R. Derwent

Robin Hood's Stride

B5056

Birchover

Wensley

Darley Dale

Hartington

Elton

Winster

B5057

MATLOCK

A5012

Steam Railway

Matlock Bath

Lead Mining Museum

High Peak Trail

Grangemill

Masson Mills

Lea Gardens

Arkwright's Mill

Tram Museum

Alstonfield

A515

Middleton Top Engine House

Cromford

Black Rocks

Crich

High Peak Junction

B5056

Bolehill

WIRKSWORTH

Carsington

Hopton Hall

A6

0   1   2 miles

0   1km

Visitor Centre

Derby

Ashbourne

B5035

Hognaston

N
W   E
S

Ancient remains

Despite the presence of limestone, the number of caves is surprisingly small, Lathkill Head Cave being the only one of any size. Early man therefore made use of the surface of the area for burial purposes and numerous tumuli can be found marked on the OS map. It is little wonder that Thomas Bateman, the nineteenth-century barrow-digger, lived in this district, at Middleton-by-Youlgreave; few of these 'lows', as they are called, escaped his attention.

The most fascinating, and of national importance, is **Arbor Low**, situated south of Monyash and just off the Youlgreave to Parsley Hay road. Now in the care of English Heritage, this huge stone circle consists of a ring of stones surrounded by a bank and ditch, the external diameter being nearly 300ft (92m). It is considered that the stones originally stood upright, although all but one have fallen, and that there were originally thirty-nine of them. Arbor Low has an evocative atmosphere. Adjacent to it is Gib Hill with an earlier henge. A Roman road runs just to the west of Gib Hill and an old trackway can be traced between the two. It would seem that the Roman surveyor made use of an already existing prehistoric trackway.

Stanton Moor, to the east, has an impressive collection of five stone circles and over seventy tumuli. The most celebrated circle is the one known as the **Nine Ladies**, which is not really a stone circle but the remains of a large barrow with the earth removed. The nine stones still stand, with a further stone, the King Stone, situated some 130ft (40m) away. To the west on Harthill Moor lies another circle, **Nine Stones**, although only four stones now survive together with the remains of an Iron Age fort, by Harthill Moor Farm. Nearby, a curious outcrop is known as **Robin Hood's Stride**; the rocks contain a small cave used as a shelter by a hermit in medieval times. It has a crucifix carved on the wall and a niche for a candle. Between the rocks and the cave is an ancient road called the Portway. This was known to be an old trackway even in Saxon times, and from the nearby fort it descended to Alport where it can easily be followed over Haddon Fields in the direction of Ashford.

A fine Anglo-Saxon artifact was found in the **Benty Grange tumulus**, just north-west of Arbor Low. Here, Thomas Bateman uncovered the burial of a warrior together with his helmet consisting of iron straps with a silver cross fixed to the nose-guard and surmounted by a bronze boar. A further remarkable find came from a barrow at Winster which yielded a cross of pure gold surmounted by a cut stone of garnet. It is richly carved and denotes the Christian influence, which was beginning to penetrate the area.

Many of the tumuli, including Benty Grange, were excavated by Thomas Bateman who lived at Lomberdale Hall near to Middleton-by-Youlgreave. It is still a private house and is not open to the public. Nearby in the village of Middleton is the Congregational Chapel, which he had built, and at the rear (also on private land but visible from the road) is his grave. Surrounded by iron railings, the grave is covered by a stone tomb surmounted by a carved stone cinerary urn similar to those he unearthed. It is a pity that his final resting place is largely forgotten.

To the south of Middleton, beyond the Newhaven to Via Gellia road, there is an archaeological trail centred on **Roystone Grange**, after which the trail is named. It starts at the Minninglow car park (by the old railway bridge over the Parwich to Pikehall road) and gives a fascinating insight into the area's history. It incorporates the old railway, a nineteenth-century brick kiln, the medieval Roystone Grange and an adjacent Roman farmhouse and field system. A leaflet on the trail is available from the National Park office at Bakewell.

Around Lathkill Dale and Bradford Dale

The area covered by this chapter includes Lathkill Dale and Bradford Dale, two of the most picturesque dales imaginable. The clear waters in themselves are a striking attraction, particularly when one has the time to watch the trout as they dart about. **Lathkill Dale** starts in an unpromising sort of way, half a mile (800m) to the east of Monyash. A footpath leaves the B5055 at the bottom of Bagshaw Dale and heads south-east towards Lathkill Dale. It is a convenient place to park the car. Soon, small outcrops of limestone give way to a narrow, deep and steep sided valley, devoid of water and with a rocky floor. After about a mile (1.6km) the river can usually be seen flowing from the mouth of a large cave

on the right known as **Lathkill Head Cave**. Despite its promising entrance it is in fact a very low cave inside for a considerable distance before passages lead down to other levels. It is also dangerous in showery weather as it is prone to flood quickly.

Further downstream, at the foot of the dry valley leading up to Haddon Grove, lie the remains of Carter's Mill. This small cornmill was intact during World War II but now only the foundations survive. Here, the valley becomes wooded and the path follows the river amid leafy glades and old lead mining ruins.

Soon after entering the wood a weir dams the river creating a small pool with the occasional duck swimming about. This pool provided a head of water for two waterwheels lower downstream; the watercourse or leat can be seen running horizontally down the valley on the far side of the river. Further on there are several collapsed shafts of the Lathkill Dale lead mine. The site of the 52ft (16m) diameter waterwheel – one of England's largest – can still be seen.

Lower downstream, the leat crossed over the valley on an aqueduct with limestone piers which have been preserved in various stages of completeness. This brought the leat to the northern side of the river where it ran to Mandale lead mine. Part of the engine house remains here, together with its associated pumping shaft which also had a waterwheel for pumping purposes. Due to its operating expense, the Cornish-type beam engine would only be used when waterpower was insufficient. Much of the valley is part of the Derbyshire

Lathkill Dale, below Over Haddon

Monyash

Dales National Nature Reserve. It is a sensitive area and visitors should not stray from the footpath. Leaflets about the reserve are available near Lathkill Lodge.

A few minute's walk from here is **Lathkill Lodge** with a mill pond and a former cornmill. Around the Lodge area the river bed is sometimes dry which spoils the river's attractiveness. Down stream, a succession of eleven weirs creates a marvellous sight when you look back at them.

From the Lodge one may climb out of the valley to **Over Haddon** or southwards up the track and across the fields to Meadow Place Grange and Youlgreave. At Over Haddon is the Lathkill, a lovely pub with memorable views down into Lathkill Dale and beyond to Youlgreave and Stanton Moor. It has a large restaurant and bar food. At the top end of Lathkill Dale, food is available at the Monyash pub, the Bull's Head. Over Haddon was the birthplace of Sir Maurice Oldfield who rose to be head of British Intelligence.

Literary connection

Raper Lodge was featured in the film *The Virgin and the Gypsy* starring Franco Nero. Also filmed was much of Youlgreave, which is referred to as Congreave in the story, written by D H Lawrence. Lawrence was no stranger to the area, for he lived for a while at Mountain Cottage, New Road, Middleton-by-Wirksworth.

The model for Ian Fleming's character 'M' in the James Bond films, he is buried at Monyash.

At Conksbury, the old packhorse bridge carrying the Bakewell to Youlgreave road is crossed before continuing down the opposite bank towards **Raper Lodge**. Surprisingly unmentioned by Pevsner, this handsome house looks down on the river and another old packhorse bridge.

Meres

The limestone plateau is an area mainly devoid of surface water. Rain water for animals and villagers was captured in clay-lined ponds known as meres. Most villages had one, usually fed by a spring or stream and many exist in open fields. Each farmer would bring his animals to drink at a specific time in the day.

Monyash had four meres, three for animals and one for domestic use. The largest, Fere Mere (shown here), still survives. Some meres are very old; for example Heathcote Mere, near Hartington, was in existence in 1482.

Local water

Youlgreave still has its own water supply from Bradford Dale and the Fountain (see below)is a reminder of when it was first installed. It has a capacity of 1,200 gallons (5460l), but is no longer used.

The river meadows soon lead to **Alport** with its seventeenth- and eighteenth-century cottages, ancient bridge, and another mill and mill pool in an idyllic setting. Nearby the Lathkill meets the Bradford and closely hugs the road before meeting the River Wye at Picory Corner.

The River Bradford commences south of Middleton-by-Youlgreave, but the dale only becomes of consequence at Middleton where a track leads down to the dale. The track is a little rough underfoot and the bare limestone outcrops and overhanging trees give nothing away of the beauty of the dale beyond, as it brings one down to an old pumping station. The beauty of **Bradford Dale** lies in the six pools of crystal-clear water reflecting the mature trees which line the sides of this steep-sided dale at its upper end, downstream of the old pumping station. The track between Middleton and the river is a mass of yellow celandines in spring.

Youlgreave spills down into the dale, but the intrusion is on the whole a sympathetic one. A clapper bridge enables one to cross the river and either proceed downstream or walk up to the village. Beyond the bridge, the path hugs the river until a road crosses the valley, which by now is getting much more shallow and open. Just beyond the road a bridge crosses the river yet again and a path follows the river down to Alport.

Youlgreave is a linear village, with its sturdy church causing a 'dog-leg' in the through road. The church displays architecture spanning 800 years, and stands in a dominating position at the end of the main street. The village is an ideal spot from which to explore the Lathkill and Bradford Dales. It was an important lead mining village and its many houses are old workers' cottages. The old Co-op, featured in *The Virgin and the Gypsy*, is now a youth hostel. It is situated opposite a large, round stone tank dated 1829 known as the Fountain.

Further down the main street to the west is the old hall, adjacent to the road. This lovely house looks similar to Hartington Hall, but is only two storeys high whilst the latter is three.

In addition to the dales there are, of course, the many villages which are scattered throughout the area, chiefly in a linear pattern on the limestone plateau. As they all have their own characteristics, space only permits a mention of some of them. In the north, **Chelmorton** lies besides a large hill, presumably on the site of a spring; it is an interesting place to explore. The oldest part of the village was obviously near to the hill and spring, which is why the church and pub now appear to be at the end of a cul-de-sac. With the coming of the first enclosure, land appears to have been allotted so that each cottage had a few strips behind it and this order has been preserved, so that even today there are many narrow fields stretching away; later enclosures resorted to a more regular pattern. One of the highest in Derbyshire, Chelmorton Church has a collection of stone coffins carved with swords, crests and even a pair of scissors.

Lead mining villages

To the south-west lies **Monyash**. It was once an important centre of the lead mining industry, with a weekly market. The old market cross still stands on the green, its base supposedly made from the old village stocks. The lead mining area of Derbyshire still has its own Barmoot Court – the oldest industrial court in the country, possibly a thousand years old. Of the four former village ponds (or 'meres') at Monyash, only Fere Mere remains. The pub is very popular with walkers and tourists, particularly in the summer as one can sit outside opposite the village green.

To the south lies **Winster**, with a similar history of dependence on lead mining, demonstrated by the discovery of a water pressure engine in a nearby mine. This engine is now re-erected in the Peak District Mining Museum in Matlock Bath. It had originally been built at Coalbrookdale in 1819 for the Alport mines, near to Youlgreave, before being moved to Winster nearly 30 years later.

Look for the **Market House** in the centre of the village, which was the first property acquired by the National Trust in Derbyshire. Pevsner describes it as being of the fifteenth or sixteenth century, but its original open ground floor arches have been built in with brick to give it more stability. It is open to the public and the National Trust maintains a small display on the first floor. In the main street lies the early Georgian hall, now a hotel.

To the north of Winster are the **Rowter Rocks** at **Birchover**, which were once thought to have connections with the Druids, hence the name of the nearby Druid Inn. Caves, rooms, steps, alcoves, armchairs, etc were carved from the rocks to form a retreat for the local vicar, the Rev Thomas Eyre, who died in 1717. However the huge 'rocking stone' no longer rocks. If you are travelling along the lane to Winster from Birchover, look out for the restored village stocks. Above the village is the old village quarry. It is still in production, supplying cut gritstone to local builders, (who are often required to build in traditional materials) plus markets further afield.

Depending on time available, a drive around some of Winster's neighbouring villages should not be overlooked. There are some delightful corners to be seen in **Stanton-in-the-Peak**, just to the north. It has an unusually named pub, the Flying Childers, named after a horse belonging to The Duke of Devonshire, purchased in 1719. A horse race at Doncaster named after him is still run annually. The stone circles and Bronze Age tumuli on Stanton Moor have already been mentioned, but look out for the Cork Stone, Cat Stone and Andle Stone – huge natural blocks of gritstone, the Cork Stone and the Andle Stone having foot-holes and iron handles for climbing to the top. The sharp-eyed visitor might find the rocks with dates and initials that were carved in the early nineteenth century by the Thornhill family of Stanton Hall. More obvious is the Earl Grey Tower, built in 1832 to celebrate the passing of the Reform Bill.

To the east on the minor road from Wensley to Matlock via Oaker Hill, lies the tiny village of **Snitterton** with its lovely Hall. There are many places of interest like these if one is prepared to seek out the backwaters.

The area now under discussion contains some of the deepest and formerly the richest lead mines in the Peak. The most notable remains are those of **Magpie Mine** near to Sheldon. They can be seen from the Monyash

to Ashford-in-the-Water road and a footpath crosses the site.

Magpie Lead Mine is situated on the limestone plateau, between Monyash and Sheldon villages, approximately 0.5 mile (0.8km) south of Sheldon. The Peak District is well known for its ancient lead-mining industry. However, it was never like the heavily mechanised mining industry in Cornwall, where ruined engine-houses litter the landscape. By comparison, very few steam engines were employed in the Peak and therefore there are fewer remains of buildings, etc.

In fact, Magpie Mine is the only major complex to survive in anything like its complete state. Magpie owes its

Stone Walls

The Peak is characterised by thousands of miles of stone walls, which were mainly built at the time of the enclosures in the eighteenth and nineteenth centuries. Some are much older and a system of Roman walls has been discovered at Roystone Grange near Parwich. Quite often the walls preserve centuries-old farming patterns. Around Hartington the walls are known to follow the lines of the old strip-fields in considerable detail, preserving the field system as marked on a map of 1614.

The walls are dry, ie built without mortar. They are, in effect, two walls the middle being filled with small stones but with plenty of large stones or throughs, to bind the whole together. They are topped by large stones called 'copers'.

A good stonewaller never puts a stone down once he has picked it up. Competitions are held annually, but it is not a spectator sport!

Pinfold, Biggin-by-Hartington

Magpie Lead Mine, near Monyash

Fere Mere, Monyash

survival to its use as a lead mine until the post-war years; it finally closed in 1958. Today, when viewed from the nearby road, it looks an impressive sight with its huge engine-house, head-gear (supporting the cage), two chimney stacks and other buildings, including a cottage. The buildings have been stabilised and are all in a good state of repair.

The site is open to visitors, but cars should be left on the road and all shafts avoided. The mine-drawing shaft is 728ft (222m) deep and many other shafts exist on the vein, or rake, which passes through the site – hence careless exploration may be hazardous even though many of the shafts have been capped for safety. The information contained in the guidebook, which is available at the Mining Museum at Matlock Bath, makes viewing the old buildings much more interesting.

The whole site is dominated, however, by the Cornish-style engine house that was built in 1824 to house a Newcomen-type steam engine with a 42in (1.07m) cylinder. This engine was replaced in 1840 by another one, built on the Cornish principle with a 40in (1m) cylinder and 36ft (11m) long boiler, which was situated in an

Flora of the mines

In midsummer, the old rake workings are a mass of flora, including bird's-foot trefoil, thyme, alpine penny-cress and ox-eye daisy. Spring sandwort is a lead-tolerant plant with five-petalled white flowerheads and is to be found in May along with early purple orchids.

adjoining building. Although it looks as though the front gable of the building is missing, this part was built tradition-ally of wood rather than stone and would have been removed to pull out the engine bob or beam that formerly sat on the wall. Behind is a circular chimney which is built of stone and finished with a brick top.

In front of the engine-house is situated the shaft itself with its steel head-gear, which replaced the wooden head-gear in 1951 when an electric winder was installed. On a lower level is a further engine-house that was built around 1870. Although its engine was scrapped in 1951, the winding drum survived, its alignment with the shaft now blocked by the new corrugated iron engine-house that was built in 1951. It is reputed to be the only listed mine building of this construction.

The cottage was built in about 1864 and has been rebuilt following a dis-astrous fire. Fortunately, the adjacent blacksmith's forge survived. A further square-built chimney survives between the forge and the 1870s' engine-house. A flue runs to the engine-house, but it may be much older, originally serving another engine half a century before. This large and complex site has an interesting history despite the fact that the lead ore extracted was not great. It is satisfying to know that the stabilisation programme has secured its future, but the site cries out for an interpretation centre, for only in this way can the te-nacity and skill of the Derbyshire lead miner be properly exhibited in situ.

Opencast mining for fluorspar occurs from time to time, often reworking the waste heaps thought worthless by the old lead miners. A bonus is that, as the sites are worked out, the land is restored to agricultural use.

A further valley worth having a look at is the **Via Gellia**. Unfortunately it now has the A5012 running down it, and is much frequented by heavy lorries. It is named after the Gell family who lived at Hopton Hall and owned much land around here. They planted the trees in the dale, for which it is well known.

Between Middleton-by-Wirksworth and Bolehill is the **National Stone Centre**. Situated on a 50 acre (20 hectares) site, there is a 'Story of Stone' exhibition from prehistoric times to the present and a Fossil Trail amid a Site of Special Scientific Interest. It also has a large selection of minerals, fossils and gemstones for sale. Trails have been set out to introduce visitors to the Peak District landscape and a special feature of that landscape, drystone walls, is highlighted by the Millennium Wall. Some 150 members of the Dry Stone Walling Association from all over Britain contributed to the wall, each in their own style and type of stone.

Between the Stone Centre and Black Rocks is the **Steeple Grange Light Railway**. This unique narrow gauge railway climbs through disused limestone quarries to Killers Dale, visitors being carried on rolling stock once used in the mines and quarries. Off the Cromford to Wirksworth road at Bolehill is the **Black Rocks Trail**. There are three woodland trails around the Black Rocks outcrop, a picnic area plus a walk on the High Peak Trail. The gritstone rocks here are popular with rock climbers.

Wirksworth

To the south of the region lies **Wirksworth**. It would be easy to dismiss it as a drab town set amid the devastation of centuries of mining and quarrying. However there has been much conservation work here in recent years and there are several interesting buildings that should be sought out. **St Mary's church** is hidden behind the shops, having access from several narrow passages. Even the main gates to the church are hemmed in between shops. The church contains a richly carved stone coffin lid of about AD800, found under the floor in 1820. Even though incomplete it depicts forty figures and is regarded as one of the most interesting early Anglo-Saxon remains in Britain. The churchyard is circular in shape – an indication of a very early Christian settlement.

A path circles the churchyard creating a backwater of peace and quiet. Walk around the north side of the church past the old Grammar School, founded in 1576 and rebuilt in 1828 in a neo-Gothic style. Its battlements and pinnacles create a pleasing elevation. It is now used for furniture manufacture. Continue past the old almshouses and turn north with the latter and the former Grammar School on your left, to emerge into Coldwell Street. On the right is the old manse, a three-storey Georgian building standing opposite the older, early seventeenth-century Manor House, hidden behind its hedge.

Near the top of Coldwell Street, towards the Market Place, a passage on the right of the United Reform Church leads into Chapel Lane. On the left, some 200yd (185m) or so up the lane, stands the **Moot Hall** which was rebuilt in 1814. It still houses the standard measure for lead ore – a bronze dish made in 1513.

After each sitting in this building of the Barmoot Court, the jury received until recently clay pipes and tobacco to smoke after their meal. At the beginning of the 21st century, Britain's oldest industrial court has most likely been sitting in three millenia.

Return to Coldwell Street past the imposing Red Lion pub and cross the main road. Have a look at Symonds House (Number 15) across the road from the Red Lion, together with the restored seventeenth-century former house behind it in Dale End. Climb up the lane to reach Babington House on the left. It is a stiff climb up Greenhill to it but the house is well worth seeing. Pevsner attributes it to the early seventeenth century, although on a modern porch is the date 1588. Near the town centre is **Wirksworth Heritage Centre** where local customs and industries are explained, along with other aspects of the town.

It is situated in an old silk and velvet mill and is staffed by volunteers. It has various exhibits: the Quarryman's Houseplace which illustrates the lifestyle of a quarryman a century ago; the local customs of well dressing and clypping the church are explained together with features on local quarrying and leadmining. A recreation of 'The Dream Cave' is portrayed where the remains of a Woolly Rhino were discovered. There is a restaurant, the Crown Yard Kitchen, attached to the centre.

Industrial Archaeology

The most noticeable industrial remains are the 100,000 or so lead mine shafts, which are to be found mainly along the worked out mineral veins. Derbyshire's lead mines were worked from Roman times, and in the seventeenth and eighteenth centuries large quantities of lead were used on the roofs of churches, country houses and other buildings. The mineral veins are often easy to identify as they frequently have a long belt of trees to act as a windbreak. The most complete mine complex is at Magpie Mine north-east of Monyash, while another ruined engine-house is at Mandale Mine in Lathkill Dale. The Peak District Mining Museum at Matlock Bath displays many artifacts and a huge pumping engine powered by water pressure, recovered from deep underground near Winster. Lead mine shafts are dangerous and one should satisfy one's curiosity about them from a safe distance.

There is plenty to interest railway enthusiasts. The world's oldest in situ piece of rail can be seen at High Peak Wharf at Cromford, together with other buildings and incline-hauling equipment. Buildings remain at the Hulme End terminus of the Leek and Manifold Light Railway. The Froghall incline, abandoned in 1920, was the second oldest line in Britain and may still be followed in places. Various other lines have been converted into trails. Railway centres exist around the Peak at Cheddleton, Foxfield, Matlock, Glossop and Butterley. The National Tramway Museum at Crich houses over forty restored trams which now operate on a mile-long (1.6km) track. Peak Rail has built its headquarters at Darley Dale and has a line extending to Rowsley, where it has excavated the old Rowsley shed.

Nearby in Matlock there was an inclined street tramway up Bank Road. It was built by George Newnes, who established *Tit Bits* magazine. Although it was closed in 1927, the depot at the top of the hill survives as does the Crown Square tram shelter which is now in the adjacent gardens.

Canals surround the Peak and survive to this day, although the Cromford Canal has been abandoned following a tunnel collapse. Canal wharfs remain at Buxworth, Whaley Bridge, Marple, Cromford and Froghall.

Stationary steam engines were usually sold off but the region is fortunate in having two preserved in situ, both open to the public. Middleton Top winding engine hauled wagons up an incline on the Cromford and High Peak Railway, while a Cornish-type beam engine worked a huge plunger pump at Leawood on the Cromford Canal.

The Peak has few water mills, although the Brindley Corn Mill at Leek and Cheddleton Flint Mill are both open to the public. Caudwell's Mill at Rowsley is a preserved roller-driven corn grinding mill which now has a craft centre and tea room. The large complex of mill buildings comprising Arkwright's Mill at Cromford is also now preserved. Unfortunately it is devoid of machinery, unlike the Paradise Silk Mill at Macclesfield where demonstrations take place on the original weaving machines. However nearby Masson Mill is now open to the public and has a museum of textile machinery. Cromford village has much else of interest including early examples of houses built by Arkwright for his workers.

Scattered along the gritstone edges above the Derwent Valley are many abandoned millstones and grindstones. Below Surprise View near Longshaw are hundreds of them, many still ready for removal along an old tramway line. On the limestone area are some very good examples of old limekilns, ranging from quite small examples built just to satisfy local needs, to large batteries of kilns, the largest being at Froghall Wharf.

Below left: Lea Wood Pumphouse, near Cromford. Below right: Brindley's Mill, Leek

Around Wirksworth

To the west of Wirksworth is **Carsington Water**, opened by HM the Queen in 1992. There is plenty to see and do at Carsington Water. In fact it is sensible to allow a full day, especially if you wish to walk around the reservoir for the path is approximately 9 miles (14.4km) in length.

The Visitor Centre has an award-winning exhibition on water and four shops offering a wide range of gifts. In addition to a quick snack bar in the courtyard, there is also the first floor Mainsail Restaurant with good views over the water. As you enter the Visitor Centre, look closely at the bulletins posted by the door – they include factual information on how much water is in the reservoir. In the summer of 1996 it was only 39% full.

Adjacent to the Visitor Centre is a watersports and cycle hire centre. Canoes, sailing dinghies and sail boards are available for hire with tuition if required. Brown trout fishing is available from April to October from the bank or from boats. There is a Carsington Bird Club and several hides along the trails around the water. The paths are well waymarked and regularly used by ramblers and cyclists.

Carsington Visitor Centre is open every day except Christmas Day. There are plenty of picnic tables and a childrens' play area near the centre. Look out for special events, especially the Country Fair in the autumn.

North of Wirksworth in the Derwent Valley lies **Cromford**, which grew as a result of the prosperous mills of Sir Richard Arkwright. Arkwright built the Greyhound Inn together with houses for his workers and a school for their children. On the south side of the road to Wirksworth, North Street was built by him and the school is situated at the end of the street. Behind the Wirksworth road and just to the east of North Street is the village lock up and the 'tail' or beginning of Cromford Sough.

Arkwright's Cromford Mill just off the A6 on the road to Lea and Holloway, is being developed as a museum and there is a shop and café here. A tour guide is available to describe the various features of this historically important mill. There is an audio-visual display and two exhibitions that tell the story of Arkwright, cotton spinning and Cromford.

It was at Cromford that Sir Richard Arkwright established the world's first water-powered cotton mill in 1772, plus **Masson Mill** built in 1783, situated alongside the A6 between Cromford and Matlock Bath. The latter still proudly displays the legend 'Sir Richard Arkwright & Co, Established 1769'. It has recently been renovated and now houses a shopping complex and a **Working Textile Museum** plus a café overlooking the river.

Down Mill Lane – the road to Crich – there are a number of other features also of interest. There is Cromford Mill with exhibits, shop and tea room set within the old cotton mill. Above the Cromford canal basin if you look across the canal basin, high above is Rock House, Arkwright's home. From the Cromford Canal wharf there is a pleasant towpath, which leads to **High Peak Wharf** with its buildings from the Cromford and High Peak Railway.

Vehicle access is via a car park off the Cromford to Lea road, where the latter turns to the left away from the Derwent Valley. A path crosses the river and runs adjacent to a sewage works to reach the canal and wharf. In the buildings here can be seen a section of the world's oldest in-situ railway line. It dates from 1828 and carries the inscription 'C&HPR'.

Just down the canal from here is the **Leawood Pumping Station**, which used to pump water from the river to the canal. It is now fully restored, including a 50in (1.27m) diameter cylinder, Cornish-type beam engine and plunger pump which is steamed periodically.

Dating from 1858, this huge engine is well worth a visit, and a worthy monument to its builders and to the time and patience of its volunteer restoration team. Ask at local information offices for details of steaming days, usually Sundays at Bank Holiday weekends and in summer.

Cromford Bridge is fifteenth-century with rounded arches on one side and pointed arches on the other! At the Cromford end is an early eighteenth-century fishing temple, almost identical with Walton and Cotton's in Beresford Dale, and the ruins of a bridge chapel. On the parapet of the bridge an inscription records the successful leaping of the parapet by a horse and rider in 1697.

Across the bridge is the entrance to **Willersley Castle**, now a Christian Guild guest house. It was built by Arkwright, but he died in 1792 prior to its completion. A coffee shop is open daily allowing a quick peep at the interior of part of the building.

The road keeps close to the river before turning towards Lea Bridge and Holloway. The latter was the home of Florence Nightingale, who lived at **Lea Hurst**, now a private house and not open to the public.

When the rhododendrons are in flower in May and June it is worth visiting **Lea Gardens**. This was an old quarry site where planting of rhododendrons and timber began over 50 years ago. Today there are over 500 different species of rhododendron. The scent of the flowers pervades the whole wood and the colours of the flowers have an amazing variety and beauty. Many of them are cultivated and for sale at the shop adjacent to the tea room. A season ticket is good value for money as the colours change throughout the summer.

To get there, go down Mill Lane at Cromford and stay on the valley road until Lea is reached. The textile mill here was opened by Florence Nightingale's family. They sold it to John Smedley, and Smedleys still own the factory. There is a factory shop on the lane which is fronted on each side by the factory buildings. This same lane leads up to a sharp bend where a turn to the right goes to Lea Gardens.

A little further up the road beyond the turn to Lea Gardens is **the Coach House** on the left. There is a craft shop as well as a tearoom and restaurant here.

Opposite is Lea Green, now a college. The road up the hill at **Holloway** affords some good views over the Derwent Valley towards the white painted Alderwasley Hall. A diversion of a mile (1.6km) or so leads to the outskirts of **Crich** and the **tramway museum** with its national collection of trams. There are over fifty vehicles including a handful from overseas. They vary from a horse-drawn Sheffield tram of 1874 to another Sheffield tram of 1950, which was the last one in the city when the service finished in 1960. The car park ticket entitles you to ride on the selection of trams, which are operated on a mile of track down the edge of a quarry.

Above, the quarry is dominated by **Crich Stand** – a monument to the Sherwood Foresters who fell in the two World Wars. When you take your tram ride, look out for the lead mining display erected by the Peak District Mines Historical Society. You can get off to look at this and take another tram back. Lead ore was smelted in the area, of course, initially in bole hearths, which required wind for draught and later in cupolas which were an early reverberatory furnace. One such cupola existed at Stone Edge about 9 miles (14km) due north of Crich. The chimney still stands and is the oldest free-standing industrial chimney in Britain, dating from about 1770.

A trip to Crich can usefully be left for a rainy day for there is plenty to see and a lot can be done even when it rains. The tram sheds can be visited as well as a museum, which is housed behind the façade of the old Derby Assembly Rooms. The Red Lion pub has been moved from Stoke-on-Trent and lovingly restored here and is open for drinks and meals. With much Victoriana preserved in a street scene, you can lose yourself in a past age and wonder how long it must be before there is a comprehensive tramway revival. There is an extensive archive available for enthusiasts and plenty of picnic opportunities. From the early beginnings of raw enthusiasm, lots of ideas and a site in a disused quarry, a very impressive visitor attraction has evolved. Here is a professionally run organisation where the dream came true.

If you have a bike, bus or car, registered prior to 1 January 1968, and are prepared to park it in the Museum's Period Street for at least two hours, the driver is admitted free. Braille guide books are available and there are wheelchair ramps, although the design of the old trams precludes the access of wheelchairs.

Crich Tramway Museum

The Matlocks

Upriver from Cromford is **Matlock Bath**, a mecca for many visitors to this area. Full of hustle and bustle, crowds and souvenir shops, it is perhaps not for

Arkwright's Mil, Cromford

Wirksworth

those who come to the Peak District for the beauty and peace of its hills and dales. The A6 becomes choked with cars on sunny Bank Holidays. Not surprisingly, there is much to see, so allow plenty of time and a full wallet. One of the interesting additions is the **Mining Museum**, run by the Peak District Mines Historical Society. The centrepiece of its exhibits is a huge water-pressure engine found in a mine at Winster. This is an interesting, not a stuffy museum, and while you follow the exhibits, children can explore simulated passages and shafts. This can be combined with a visit to **Temple Mine,** worked for fluorite and lead, which gives an authentic insight into life underground.

A dramatic addition to the attractions at Matlock Bath opened at Easter 1984. Now visitors can take a cable car ride up to the **Heights of Abraham**, which gives a spectacular and unique view of the Derwent Valley. The cable car station is a little upstream of Matlock Bath Railway Station. It is easy to locate by looking for the cables slung over the A6 and the River Derwent. At the top the more energetic can visit the Great Rutland and the Great Masson Caverns. The Rutland Cavern (actually an old mine not a cave) has a very good display involving a model of an old miner and a guide who explains working conditions in the mine. Others may prefer to stroll around the woodland walks. There are two play areas for children and plenty of refreshment.

Elsewhere in the town there is **Gulliver's Kingdom** for young children, a theme park specifically aimed at 2-13 year olds. There is a good range of shops, a promenade above the river and a railway station. Each year, Matlock Bath has its illuminations with illuminated floats on the river and a firework display. More details on dates can be obtained from the information office next to the Mining Museum.

Matlock Bath Aquarium is housed in the Matlock Bath Hydro, which dates from 1883. The thermal pool, fed by a spring on the hillside, is at a constant temperature of 20°C (68°F) and is much appreciated by the collection of carp that swims there. The old consulting rooms house a collection of British and tropical freshwater fish while visitors can also enjoy the petrifying well, a hologram gallery and a collection of gemstones and fossils.

Just to the left of the aquarium is **Life in a Lens**, a museum of popular photography. Themed rooms show how photography has progressed from the early days, all set in a renovated Victorian house.

A further new addition to the attractions here is the **Whistlestop Visitor Centre**, in some of the old railway buildings (built in 1849 in a Swiss Chalet style) adjacent to the station. The main former Midland Railway station building may be seen and the old goods building has been converted to an educational centre. The shop incorporates an exhibition on the Derbyshire Wildlife Trust.

Upstream from Matlock Bath railway station are the **High Tor Grounds** – 60 acres (24 hectares) in extent with walks and views down into the Derwent Valley, with the river nearly 400ft (123m) below. Access is from Dale Road or Church Street, Matlock, or just upriver from Matlock Bath railway station.

A little south of Matlock Bath is the **New Bath Hotel**. Most people tend to regard it as being purely residential, but this is not so. When you begin to flag a little in Matlock Bath, it is an excellent choice for coffee and biscuits. Matlock itself is a good shopping centre, but it lacks the architectural appeal for example of Buxton, Bakewell or Ashbourne. Fortunately its shops are on the flat, for much of the town itself overlooks the river.

An unusual attraction in Matlock is the **Abbey Brook Cactus Nursery**. It has over 4,000 different species of cacti and succulents on display and for sale contained in four glasshouses. The nursery is the leading supplier to garden centres in the United Kingdom. There is a fascinating variety of cacti of which many are scented and some display unusually large flowers. Entry to the show house of giant cacti is free. Going towards Bakewell from Matlock the nursery is situated near the Whitworth Hospital. Turn off the A6 by Robert Young's Garden Centre off Old Hackney Lane.

Matlock developed as a spa town and many hydros, or more correctly hydropathic establishments, were built in the mid-nineteenth century. The last major hydro to survive was Smedley's, which finally closed its doors in 1955. It is a massive structure and is worth having a look at. It is now the County Council Offices and was built by John Smedley, who also built Riber Castle. The future of Riber Castle is uncertain at the time of writing. Overlooking the valley, it is a great local landmark but

since the closure of the wildlife park that was housed there, no definite plans have been agreed for its future.

In addition to the Cromford Canal, there was also a railway in the valley as far as Rowsley, where it headed up the Wye at the Duke of Devonshire's insistence that Chatsworth had to be spared the intrusion of a railway. Today it has been restored from Matlock to Rowsley South, with an intermediate station at Darley Dale. **Peak Rail** run trains, some steam and some diesel, on Sundays throughout the year and on other days during the summer and school holidays. Special events such as the Warring Forties weekend, Hallowe'en specials and Santa specials are held. Take afternoon tea on the train or stop at the tea room at Darley Dale station. There is a railway book shop at the Matlock terminus and a gift shop at Rowsley.

Matlock formerly had a tramway and a couple of trams used to run up and down the steep hill (Bank Road) between the Crown Square roundabout and Smedley's Hydro, now the County Council Offices. The tramway was closed down in 1927 and the tram shelter, which stood on the site of the roundabout, was moved to the adjacent gardens where it can still be seen.

Between Matlock and Rowsley is the **Red House Stables Carriage Museum**. Here one may browse around one of the country's finest collections of horsedrawn vehicles. There are over forty of them together with harness and equipment rooms. The museum offers scenic tours by coach and four-in-hand, plus driving tuition for which prior booking is needed.

Tufa Cottage, Via Gellia, near Cromford

Darley Dale station, north of Matlock

Places to Visit

Wirksworth and around

Winster Market House (N.T.)
Winster
Open: Apr–Sep daily
National Trust information room housing scale model of Winster village

National Stone Centre
Porter Lane, Middleton-by-Wirksworth, Matlock, Derbyshire DE4 4LS
☎ 01629 824833
www.nationalstonecentre.org.uk
Open: all year. Free access to site and trails, small charge for entry to exhibition.
50 acres (20 hectares) site telling the story of stone from prehistoric times to present.
Ⓟ 👪 free to site

Steeple Grange Light Railway
Porter Lane, Middleton
☎ 01629 580917 or 07769 802587
www.steeplegrange.co.uk
Open: 12noon-5pm Easter weekend, Sun and Bank Holidays, Apl to Oct and Sat in Jul–Sept.
Shop and light refreshments available.

Wirksworth Heritage Centre
Crown Yard DE4 4ET
☎ 01629 825225
www.storyofwirksworth.co.uk
Open: Easter–end-Sept; Wed–Sun 10.30–4.30 (inc. Bank Holidays and Oct half-term) Sun 1.30-4.30pm.
Local customs and industries explained, with recreation of the life of a quarryman in the early 1900s. Computer game and Dream Cave for children. Restaurant.
Ⓟadjacent 👪 ☀

Carsington Water Visitor Centre
Big Lane, Ashbourne DE6 1ST
Off B5035 Ashbourne to Wirksworth road ☎ 01629 540696
www.moretoexperience.co.uk
Open: from 10am daily (not Xmas Day). Apl–Sept, 10am–6pm, Oct–Mar 10am–5pm.
Visitor centre, restaurant, walks, cycle hire, bird hides, watersports.
Ⓟ ♿ 👪free ☀

Cromford

Arkwright's Cromford Mill
Mill Lane, Cromford, Matlock, Derbyshire DE4 3RQ.
On minor road leading to Lea and Holloway, 200yd (185m) east of Cromford crossroads on A6.
☎ 01629 823256
Open: daily 9am–5pm; Closed 25th Dec.
The world's first successful water-powered cotton spinning mill, now owned by the Arkwright Society and undergoing restoration. Exhibitions, audio-visual display and guided tours available.

Masson Mill
A6 near Cromford
☎ 01629 760208
www.masson-mill.co.uk
Open: daily, 10am–4pm Mon–Fri, 11am–5pm Sat, 11am–4pm Sun. Closed 25th December and Easter Day.
Shopping complex, café.

Places to Visit

Working Textile Museum

Masson Mill, Derby Rd, Matlock Bath DE4 3PY
☎ 01629 581001
Open: 10am-4pm Mon–Fri, 11am–5pm Sat, 11am–4pm Sun.
Best preserved example of one of Arkwright's cotton mills.
ⓟ ♿mostly ♨ ☀

High Peak Junction Workshops

Signposted off A6 in Cromford
☎ 01629 822831
www.derbyshire.gov.uk/countryside
Open: Summer daily 10.30am–5.30pm; Winter Sat and Sun only, 10.30am–4pm (times may vary).
Restored railway workshops of Cromford and High Peak railways. Display, video, model working forge, shop.
♿little interest for <12yrs ♨

Leawood Pumping Station

Cromford Canal DE4 5GH
☎ 01629 823204
Open: Sun–Monday of Bank Holiday weekends and Sat and Sun of the first weekend in the month in Jun, Jul, Aug and Oct.
1849 beam engine, fully restored and steamed periodically.

Lea Gardens

DE4 5GH
☎ 01629 534380
www.leagarden.co.uk
Open: daily 10am-5.30pm, mid-Mar–end-Jun.
A rare collection of rhododendrons, azaleas, alpines and conifers in a lovely woodland setting. Plants for sale. Tea shop.
ⓟ ♨<16

Crich Tramway Village

Nr Matlock DE4 5DP
☎ 01773 854321
www.tramway.co.uk
Open: Daily 10am-5.30pm, c. late Mar–end-Oct, ring at other times.
Collection of about fifty trams from home and overseas. Unlimited rides on a mile (1.6km) of tram tracks. Period buildings, exhibition, workshops.
ⓟ ♿ ♨<16 ☀

The Matlocks

Peak District Mining Museum

The Pavilion, Matlock Bath DE4 3NR
☎ 01629 583834
www.peakmines.co.uk
Open: daily except 25 Dec, 11am–3pm, 10am–5pm in summer(may close later at busy times in summer)
Trevithick's giant water pressure engine. Climbing shafts and tunnels. Displays of geology, minerals and mining in the Peak District since Roman times. Shop selling souvenirs, specialist mining books and local interest books.
ⓟ ♿ ♨great for kids ☀

Temple Mine

Near mining museum
Details of visits may be obtained from the Peak District Mining Museum at Matlock Bath.
☎ 01629 583834
Underground experience of an early 20th century lead and fluorspar mine.

Heights of Abraham

Adjacent to Matlock Bath railway station DE4 3PD
☎ 01629 582365
www.heightsofabraham.com
Open: Phone or check website for details. Cablecar; Great Masson Cavern and Pavilion; Visitors' Centre; Victoria Prospect Tower; Great Rutland Cavern and Nestus Mine; Alpine Centre.

Ⓟ ♿ ♨<16

Gulliver's Kingdom

Temple Walk, Matlock Bath, turn up the hill to the south of and opposite the Pavilion
☎ 01925 444888
www.gulliversfun.co.uk
Open: daily, Easter–Oct, 10.30am–5pm; weekends only early and late season. Party rates available. Theme park and rides for 2-13 year olds.

Ⓟ ♿in part, steep inclines ♨child rate for <90cm high ☛

Matlock Bath Aquarium

North Parade, DE4 3NS
☎ 01629 583624
Open: daily Easter–end-Oct; 10am–5.30pm. Winter 10am–5pm, weekends only.
Freshwater aquarium, hologram gallery and gemstone and fossil collection.

Life in a Lens

North Parade, Matlock Bath, DE4 3NS
☎ 01629 583325
Open most week days 11am-5.30pm. Occasional opening at weekends.

High Tor

Access from near Matlock Bath station, Church Street or Dale Road, Matlock or from Starkholmes

Open: daily, 10am-dusk
Explore old Roman lead workings, 60 acres (24 hectares) of grounds, woodland walks, children's playground and café.

Abbey Brook Cactus Nursery

Old Hackney Lane, Matlock DE4 2QJ
☎ 01629 580306
Open: 1-4pm Wed–Fri, 1–5pm Sat and Sun. Open Bank Holiday Mondays.
Over 4,000 different species of cacti and succulents on display and for sale. Tearoom available at Robert Young's adjacent nursery.

Ⓟ ♿ ♨free ☛

Peak Rail

Matlock Station DE4 3NA
☎ 01629 580381
www.peakrail.co.uk
Open: weekends and Bank Holidays all year round and midweek during the summer months.
Enjoy a nostalgic trip up the River Derwent Valley, north of Matlock, pulled by steam. Relax in the leisurely atmosphere of the 'Palatine' licensed restaurant car — and enjoy a meal with a difference. Party bookings welcome.

Ⓟ ♿ ♨

Red House Stables
Carriage Museum

Darley Dale, Matlock DE4 2ER
☎ 01629 733583
www.workingcarriages.com
Open: daily from 10am
Over forty horse-drawn vehicles, equipment and harness rooms.

Ⓟ ♿ ♨

4. The Northern Limestone Plateau

The River Wye rises on Axe Edge and flows down to Buxton before turning eastwards to divide the limestone region into two. Much of its course north of Rowsley is followed by the A6 trunk road. The valley has two quite distinct features. North-west of Bakewell it is narrow and deeply incised with sheer limestone bluffs which in places even overhang the river. It is joined by many tributary valleys, mostly quite deep but chiefly devoid of water. The largest are Great Rocks Dale, the two Deep Dales, Monk's Dale, Tideswell Dale, Cressbrook Dale and Taddington Dale. South-east of Bakewell, the river flows across softer, younger rocks which have eroded more easily creating a wider valley.

Fortunately, the A6 road took advantage of Taddington Dale and so spared perhaps the most beautiful part of the Wye, between Topley Pike and the bottom of Monsal Dale. Part of this can be viewed from the car, but much is preserved for the rambler, including the most interesting parts of Chee Dale, Water-cum-Jolly Dale and parts of Monsal Dale.

North of the Wye, the limestone plateau is dissected by some of the tributary valleys mentioned above. The limestone upland stretches as far north as Castleton and Eyam (which are included in Chapter 5) and includes some minor hills such as Longstone Edge, Bradwell Moor and Eldon Hill. It is an area of dry-stone walls and dry valleys

The Northern Limestone Plateau

0   1   2 miles

0   1km

Great Hucklow

Grindleford

Foolow

Eyam Hall

B6054

Litton

A623

Eyam

Tideswell

Wardlow

Froggatt

Monk's Dale

Cressbrook Dale

Tideswell Dale

Stoney Middleton

Calver

Wormhill

Miller's Dale

Chee Dale

Curbar

BUXTON

B6465

R. Derwent

B6001

Hassop

Baslow

Monsall Trail

Topley Pike

Taddington

A6

Gt Longstone

Fin Cop

Chatsworth

Chelmerton

Taddington Dale

Monsall Dale

R. Wye

A619

Edensor

N

W   E

S

Ashford-in-the-Water

BAKEWELL

Beeley

A515

B5055

A6

Haddon Hall

B6012

Monyash

Rowsley

with dairy and sheep farms. It has also been an important area for quarrying and lead mining.

Background

The area was of importance to man in early times. When the Romans arrived they found a small, but presumably effective, system of Iron Age forts and connecting routes. The ancient Portway which came north from Derby crossed through the area. From Wirksworth, the road headed via Grangemill for Castle Ring, an Iron Age fort north-west of Winster above Robin Hood's Stride. From there, it made for Alport and crossed the high ground west of Bakewell before descending to the village of Ashford-in-the-Water where it forded the Wye. It is easy to see the Portway at Ashford descending down to the river opposite Ashford Hall. Ashford was an important crossing place for the River Wye and the ancient Portway was used for centuries as a major highway. Indeed, north of the village, it is now surfaced and is still in use as part of the road to Wardlow and Foolow.

The importance of Ashford is reflected in the establishment of a castle north of the church, although nothing now remains except for a few place names including Castle-gate, the current name for the Portway north of the village. From Ashford, the Portway proceeded to Monsal Head along the existing roadway and then on to Wardlow Mires where it probably branched, heading through the fields to an Iron Age camp at Burr Tor close to the gliding club, and then on to Bradwell via Robin Hood's Seat. The alternative route from Wardlow Mires took a more direct route to Bradwell via Windmill.

Somewhere along the road between Ashford and Monsal Head, a track would have branched off to the west to the Iron Age fort at the top of the promontory known as Fin Cop. There is no public right of way to the fort but the site can be best appreciated from the west of the River Wye. Fin Cop is visible for a considerable distance, and with its two very steep sides at almost right angles to each other it would have presented a visually impressive and physically important defensive position. Of great antiquity even in Iron Age times were the tumuli and stone circles. Just to the north of Tideswell is Tideslow, the largest tumulus in the Peak District.

Perhaps of more interest is Five Wells, unfortunately off the right-of-way just north of the farm of that name situated on the path between Chelmorton and Taddington, as it crosses Sough Top. Five Wells is a chambered burial tomb from the Bronze Age which was uncovered during excavation. At 1,400ft (431m) it is the highest cairn in the country. Relics from here and other prehistoric sites can be seen in Buxton Museum.

Buxton

Buxton itself has an ancient history. It attracted the Romans because of its warm mineral water which bubbles up to the surface. They built a bath here and called their settlement *Aquae Arnemetiae*. To the bath came Roman roads from Derby, Leek, Brough (*Navio*) east of Castleton, and south from near Glossop from a fort probably called *Ardotalia* but more popularly known by the fictitious *Melandra*. Other roads came from the west and the north-west. A Roman milestone found in 1856 is now preserved in the museum.

After the Romans left, the spring was not entirely forgotten and by Tudor times it had a reputation for curing invalids. Mary Queen of Scots whilst a prisoner in the custody of William, Earl of Shrewsbury, came here to seek relief from rheumatism. The spa waters rise from underground at a temperature of 82°F (27°C).

St Anne's Well, opposite the Crescent still produces spring water and many local people come daily to collect their drinking supplies, preferring the well to their local tap water. The **Pump Room**, close to the well, currently houses an exhibition of local arts and crafts during the summer months, enabling public access at the same time.

The Crescent built adjacent to the spring was designed by John Carr of York for the fifth Duke of Devonshire. It was built between 1780 and 1790 and was the first important imitation of the Royal Crescent at Bath, as part of a deliberate plan by the Duke to build Buxton into a spa town to rival that city. According to Pevsner, it cost £38,000, which means it could have been financed out of a single year's sales from the Ecton Mine in the Manifold Valley, as is traditionally believed. It was built primarily as a hotel and shopping complex and was partly occupied from 1786. At the north end was the Great Hotel, until 1993 the public library.

Recent detective work has revealed that the Old Hall – used by Mary Queen of Scots and other wealthy visitors to Buxton's Elizabethan Spa – still survives. It was built as a four-storey tower house and is depicted as such on Speed's map of 1610.

Standing to the left of the Crescent is the current **Old Hall Hotel**. The original building has been extended to both the front and rear. Look for the part with the bay windows. The original floor level is below the current road level, but the four storeys can be easily seen. The principal bedroom in this section is still known as the Queen of Scots Room. The full story of the discovery can be read in the 1994 Journal of the Derbyshire Archaeological Society.

After the building of the Crescent, patronage by the Devonshire family continued with the building of the stables to the rear of the Crescent during 1785-90. This was converted to the **Devonshire Royal Hospital** in 1859, and the central courtyard previously used for exercising the horses was covered with a dome in 1881-2. At the time, it was the largest dome in the world, being 156ft (48m) in diameter and weighing 560 tons! The hospital

has now closed but it is now possible to see inside this building again as it has a restaurant run by the University of Derby.

The old village parish church of Buxton is St Ann's in Upper Buxton, dating from 1625. When the Duke of Devonshire started to develop the village into a fashionable spa, it had no other church and indeed, no hotels. There were three hotels within the Crescent, after its completion. However, the new church was built in 1811, by Sir Jeffrey Wyattville, and it is situated near the Pavilion.

Adjoining the Crescent were the thermal and natural baths; the latter at the south end and the former at the northern end. The thermal baths have been converted into a shopping complex, retaining some features of the old baths. Behind the Crescent are the **Pavilion, Opera House** and **Pavilion Gardens**. The gardens and Conservatory are worth a visit, as is the restored Opera House, which has a high reputation for the quality of its performances. The Buxton Festival is held annually during July.

The Opera House was built in 1903 and retains its wonderful interior. It was built adjacent to the Pavilion, which dates from 1871. Across the road from the Opera House, lovers of street furniture will appreciate the Victorian post box. The large concert hall next to the Pavilion was added in 1875. The entrance to the Conservatory is to the left of the main entrance to the Opera House and was refurbished in the early 1980s. The area beyond the Conservatory suffered from an arson attack and has been remodelled internally with a

Pavilion Gardens in Autumn, Buxton

The Opera House, Buxton

Derby University, Buxton

Buxton's summer festivals

In the middle of the summer, this lovely Georgian spa town is host to a series of festivals, catering for both national and regional audiences and ensuring that Buxton is the liveliest place to be in high summer.

Buxton Well Dressing Festival
Information: ☎ 01298 24201

Starts the summer celebrations. Wells in Buxton are dressed and blessed in inter-denominational services on the second Wednesday in July. The process of dressing the wells can be seen in the Paxton Suite, Pavilion Gardens, on the previous two days. Procession through the streets on the following Saturday.

Buxton Festival
Mid-late July.
Information: ☎ 01298 70395
www.buxtonfestival.co.uk
Box Office: ☎ 0845 127 2190

Two-week festival offering opera, classical music and literary events. Productions of rarely seen operas by mainstream composers in the charming Edwardian opera house. Daily programme of events includes opera, concerts, talks, cabaret, lunchtime recitals, walks, public master-classes, festival masses in St John's Church and literary lectures, held in splendid venues throughout the town.

Buxton Fairs & Events
Tel: 01298 23114
www.paviliongardens.co.uk

Buxton Festival Fringe
Mid-late July.
Information: ☎ 01298 73461 (during festival only) At other times
☎ 01663 765561/01298 79351
www.buxtonfringe.org.uk
Running alongside the Buxton Festival, the Fringe presents a packed programme of drama, music, comedy, dance, spoken work - in venues all over Buxton; open to all-comers with a full range of entertainment by professional, amateur and student groups; half- and one-day arts workshops during the festival period.

The International Gilbert & Sullivan Festival
Late July and early August.
Information and Box Office:
☎ 0845 127 2190
www.gs.festival.co.uk

International Competition comprising competitive amateur performances under the scrutiny of an expert adjudicator; the Gilbert & Sullivan Opera Company, performing full-scale productions on stage in the Opera House; a festival production – from audition to stage in just one week; fringe events; concerts; recitals; workshops; master-classes; and a children's festival production.

pleasant café on the first floor looking out over the gardens and restaurant below. Beyond the Concert Hall is a modern swimming pool (filled with thermal mineral water) and adjacent car park.

There are several attractions for young children in the Pavilion Gardens, which are most attractive in the summer. The gardens have undergone considerable renovation. Owing to the town's altitude, spring arrives late and sometimes you can see daffodils and tulips in flower in the gardens in June!

The **Buxton Museum and Art Gallery** in Terrace Road includes archaeological remains found locally and from the Manifold Valley. There are also fine examples of objects made of Blue John stone from Castleton and Black Marble from Ashford-in-the-Water. Of special note are the excellent dioramas showing life in prehistoric times – complete with sound effects. The study of Sir William Boyd-Dawkins has been recreated in the museum, set out as it would have appeared some 100 years ago. There is much else to see in Buxton. A walk down Spring Gardens, the main shopping street, is recommended. The town, one of the highest in England, has a railway station, good bus services and municipal conveniences such as the Pavilion Gardens, bowling greens and two golf clubs.

Off Spring Gardens, an indoor shopping centre has been developed with adjacent car park. Access to it is from the new road that runs past the railway station. A further innovative shopping complex has been developed at the former Thermal Baths adjacent to the Crescent. It gives a good idea of what the Baths must have looked like, and the original chair in which arthritic patients could be lowered into the water has been preserved. There is a café on the first floor.

Despite the demise of its status as a spa town, Buxton is still a very pleasant town to visit and explore. South of the town, on Grin Low, is **Solomon's Temple**. This folly was built to provide labour for out-of-work men. It was restored a few years ago at a cost of £25,000 and can be reached from Poole's Cavern (off Green Lane). It is worth visiting if only for the panoramic view over Buxton.

Poole's Cavern is the only show cave on the west side of the Peak and is easy to walk through. It is beneath Grin Plantation, a wooded area planted on old lime ash tips. The huge mounds of lime ash consolidated into a kind of soft rock. In the late eighteenth century at least ten hovels had been carved out of the ash, housing poor workers employed at the limekilns.

During his tour of Britain, Daniel Defoe visited Buxton and was most impressed by Poole's Cavern. Although he did not mention these hovels in his *Tour of Britain*, he did visit some which were similar on Brassington Moor. Defoe, incidentally, was not very impressed with the accommodation available in Buxton. One suspects he would be today, for there are now numerous hotels and guest houses.

Limestone from Grin Quarry was burnt to produce lime and the waste was dumped in large quantities. Percolating ground waters have carried the lime down into the cave and this has helped produce the large number of

Above: Pavilion Gardens and (left) hanging baskets adorn the Pavilion

Monsal Head Viaduct and the Monsal Trail (opposite)

beautiful stalagmites and stalactites.

Adjacent to the Cavern is the **Buxton Country Park** set in 100 acres (40 hectares). There is a nature trail, free car park and picnic area, toilets and shop at the Cavern. A recent development is the **Go Ape! High Wire Forest Adventure** at the Cavern. Trek through treetops via rope bridges, Tarzan swings and zip slides, up to 35ft (11m plus) above the ground. Three hours of fun and adventure for the young. Minimum age: 10 years and minimum height 1.4m. Close by, on the south side of the A53 is **Buxton Raceway**, which offers a very different kind of entertainment – banger racing. There are regular meetings at weekends including some world championship qualifying rounds.

North of Buxton

Northwards lies the high moorland of Combs Moss and Shining Tor; to the south-west is Axe Edge, and south-eastwards can be seen Sough Top and the green fields and grey walls of the White Peak. The neat fields and clumps of trees of the limestone area contrast vividly with the rugged treeless moors of the western edge of the Peak.

North-west of Buxton, at **Whaley Bridge**, is the basin of the **Peak Forest Canal**, where an old warehouse, limekilns etc remain. Canal enthusiasts should visit the imposing staircase locks at **Marple Bridge** where there are more warehouses, while at the bottom of the locks is a large aqueduct some 80ft (25m) high over the River Goyt. The **Goyt Trail** starts at the Whaley Bridge basin along the canal towpath. West of Whaley Bridge is Kettleshulme, where the **Dunge Valley Gardens** are open to the public. They feature rhododendrons and bog gardens in a woodland setting.

The Wye Valley

The northern portion of the lime-stone region has many similarities to the area south of the Wye Valley. A rolling landscape of green fields with an intricate system of dry-stone walls is synonymous with the Peak District limestone region as a whole. Other than the River Wye itself, the area is devoid of any river system. It is, of course, bounded in the east by the River Derwent.

There are no counterparts for the river systems of the Dove, Manifold, Lathkill and its smaller tributary, the Bradford. The most interesting dale therefore is that of the Wye. It is crossed by a road at Miller's Dale, there is a minor road to Litton, and a road to Cressbrook and Wardlow Mires drops into the dale at Monsal Head. A little further south, the A6 runs up the valley to the bottom of Taddington Dale and returns to it for the section between Topley Pike and Buxton. There is much to see on foot and fortunately the linear pattern of the valley can be overcome by catching a bus back to one's start-ing point if the need arises. Buses run between Buxton and both Tideswell (for Sheffield) and Bakewell (for Derby and Chesterfield).

Topley Pike (SK103725) offers a good place to start. One can park oppo-site Tarmac's quarry at this point, where a minor road turns down to the river. It is marked on the OS White Peak map. This track follows the river down to the bottom of **Great Rocks Dale**, where ICI's quarry has the longest working face in Europe. The track passes through well-wooded surroundings, sharing the narrow valley with the railway which crosses three times overhead. Upon reaching the footbridge and the row of cottages – presumably built for workers of the disused quarry behind – one also leaves Wye Dale for Chee Dale. Below here, the dale becomes much more interesting and, in wet weather, even adventuresome!

For most of the way, the path in hugs the river. In places it becomes precipitous, particularly where it runs on the south side of the river near to the railway arch, and also just upstream from the tributary Flag Dale. The valley is characterised in places by sheer lime-stone bluffs, several of which overhang the valley bottom. In two places, this forces the path into the river and onto stepping stones. If the river is in flood, the dale can be impassable. The out-crops of limestone, some with sheer waterworn slabs and overhangs, offer considerable sport to climbers. The valley is well wooded in places, which offers some variety of scenery. It would be easy to overstate the scenery of the dale, but if you sometimes get bored with the near-regularity of the beauty and riverside paths in some of the other dales, remember Chee Dale.

Beyond Flag Dale, the valley opens out a little as one approaches the foot-bridge carrying the path from Wormhill to Blackwell over the river. Beyond here it is just a short walk into Miller's Dale. In former days Miller's Dale was locally an important place. It not only served as a railway station for many surrounding villages including Tideswell, but Man-chester to Derby through-trains stopped here to pick up passengers from Buxton. The passenger traffic, together with the limestone traffic, made Miller's Dale a big station for its location. The Tideswell to Taddington road also crosses the valley here and river, road and railway are neighbours yet again. There are two quite impressive railway bridges situated side by side, the initial bridge being augmented in 1903 by the second one, 40 years after the line opened.

There used to be a cornmill opposite the Angler's Rest Inn, but the waterwheel has now been reinstated at the cornmill in Cromford. A mill has been located here since at least 1767, when it had two wheels. Monk's Dale reaches the Wye Valley close by.

Commerce also dictated a road down the dale at this point to serve **Litton Mill**. Originally it was a waterwheel-driven cotton mill, and textile manufacturing has only recently ceased. The mill earned a reputation for the unfortunate excesses of child labour in the early nineteenth century, epitomised in Walter Unsworth's novel *The Devil's Mill*. The path down the dale proceeds through the millyard, at which point the road ends. The current mill dates from 1874 when a fire destroyed the earlier mill of 1782.

Beyond here lies **Water-cum-Jolly Dale**. One wonders whether the impounded water, backing up from Cressbrook Mill, inspired the name or whether it dates from a time prior to this. On a summer's day, the broad expanse of water with the waterworn limestone bluff behind reflecting in the millpool and the occasional duck or moorhen on the surface, adds to the tranquillity of the dale.

Cressbrook Mill no longer operates.

The main four-storey structure, which dates from 1815, replaced an earlier mill built by Arkwright in 1779. Of interest is his apprentice house by the mill race, looking like a Gothic castle with narrow lancet windows and turrets. Today this elegant mill crowned by a cupola has been converted to apartments.

Part of the site was previously used as a peppermint distillery using wild mint growing on nearby hillsides. This surely must rank as one of the most unusual of local occupations. It reminds one of the watercress formerly grown in Gradbach millpond for sale in Macclesfield Market, and the ropes that were made inside Peak Cavern at Castleton.

Downstream from the mill the path follows the lane to **Monsal Head**. Take not the first bridge across the river, but the second, situated where the road begins to rise towards Monsal Head. The path goes through the arches, which carried the railway line to Buxton from Bakewell. Ruskin stongly objected to the intrusion of the railway, but the line has mellowed into the landscape and the viewpoint from Monsal Head is now, ironically, well known and popular with photographers. Just downstream from the railway arches the River Wye tumbles over a weir, which many people must recognise from the numerous postcards and calendars in which it features. From here the path cuts through the meadows at the bottom of the wood to meet the A6 at the foot of **Taddington Dale** where there is a picnic site, car park and toilets.

Below Taddington Dale, the river meanders slowly to Ashford-in-the-Water and Bakewell. A footpath follows

A Walk from Bakewell

Total distance about 6 miles (9.6km) A walk with plenty of interest north of Bakewell. Park near Holme Bridge at SK215690 and take the path to the rear of Lumford Cottages. It climbs up through a small plantation adjacent to Holme Bank Chert Mine before cutting across the fields in the direction of Great Longstone. Just north of the little cottage known as Cracknowle House, the path leaves the fields and descends through Cracknowle Wood to Rowdale house and the A6020 from Ashford-in-the-Water to Hassop Station.

Turn left towards Ashford and walk along the road to the junction of the various roads adjacent to the old railway bridge. There is an access road from this junction to Churchdale Farm and on towards Churchdale Hall. The path skirts around the plateau and then drops down a hillside to rejoin the A6020. Walk down the footpath at the side of the road and turn left onto the old and now disused section of the B6465. This has now been re-routed and crosses the River Wye over a new bridge. Upon reaching the A6 a path cuts across the

Below: Holme Bridge, Bakewell

fields on your left and to the north of the A6. There are views towards Ashford Hall and down onto Ashford Lake which runs into the large mill pond of Lumford Mill. This has created quite an elongated and interesting sheet of water in the valley below the path.

Eventually one walks towards a group of houses and the path cuts through the middle of the development to join the A6 once more close to Lumford Mill. There is a short walk down the path at the side of the A6 to Holme Bridge. Here the former sheepwash has been restored and there is an interpretation board that details changes made to the river over the centuries to provide water both for Lumford and Victoria Mills.

Peak Forest and the dry dale to Miller's Dale

There is a 10 mile (16km) path which enables the walker to enjoy the variety offered in a somewhat dry, ie riverless, Derbyshire dale and also on the limestone plateau above it. Park at Peak Forest (SK115792) and take the path which leads towards Dam Dale Farm and into Dam Dale. The path continues on down a rather long valley which heads towards the River Wye at Miller's Dale. It has several names after leaving Dam Dale, the next is Hay Dale followed by Peter Dale and Monk's Dale. Parts of this valley system are now part of English Nature's Derbyshire Dales National Nature Reserve.

Great care should be taken not to interfere with the wildlife or stray from the footpath. Upon reaching Miller's Dale, just beyond the church a track leads off uphill. It is marked unsuitable for motor vehicles. After climbing out of the valley and above Monk's Dale Farm it joins an old green lane that runs directly to Wheston. Part of it has been tarmaced but the rest is comfortable walking. The road continues north-west of Wheston in the direction of Peak Forest. At SK128778 a track leads off to the left. A footpath is soon reached that should be taken back into Dam Dale towards Dam Dale Farm and Peak Forest.

Around Tideswell

From Tideswell take the road west towards Tunstead and, after descending into the top of Monk's Dale (which is now a nature reserve), a path cuts up through the fields to Wormhill reaching the village by the church. At the southern end of the village, at SK124739, take the path which heads south and then south-eastwards descending into Chee Dale. Follow the path downstream to Miller's Dale and then take the riverside road to Litton Mill. Just before the mill, turn up Tideswell Dale, beneath the grounds of Ravenstor Youth Hostel. On reaching the B6049 walk the last mile or so up the road into Tideswell. Total distance about 7 miles (11.2km).

much of the route, passing through **Great Shacklow Wood,** emerging by the river close to where the water flowing down Magpie Sough reaches the Wye. The sough (pronounced 'suff') drains Magpie Mine, situated over a mile (1.6km) away south of Sheldon village.

The entrance or sough-tail is new and gated. Some ten million gallons (45 millionL) of water per day has been recorded as flowing into the River Wye from the sough.

The path is an easy walk amid a leafy glade, reaching the fields by an old watermill. There are three water-wheels here; two are attached to an old saw mill, which was used to produce bobbins and wooden spindles for Sir Richard Arkwright's nearby cotton mills (in Cressbrookdale, Bakewell and Cromford). A third and much smaller one was used to pump water up to Sheldon village before mains water was laid.

After a short walk through the fields, the path reaches **Kirkdale** and the road to Sheldon. The works depot at Kirkdale used to be a marble mill and many of the black marble slabs visible in Derbyshire churches were cut and polished here. The stone, really a dark limestone that takes a high polish and looks like marble, was mined from two localities nearby. The marble works lost some of its buildings when the Ashford bypass was built.

Ashford-in-the-Water is worth a look around, particularly to view the old packhorse bridge – **Sheepwash Bridge** – and its neighbouring pump shelter, although the village pump has now gone. The village was once of at least equal importance to Bakewell, but that has all now changed. As early as the seventeenth century, 300 packhorses, laden with malt, passed northwards through the village each week. The bypass, constructed in 1931, took away much of the traffic. The Sheepwash Bridge was built in the seventeenth century and the sheepwash remains on the far side from the village.

In the church are some paper garlands hanging in memory of girls who died unmarried. There are also some memorials in the local black marble. The mines are on either side of the valley at the western end of the village, but should not be entered. At the western end of Ashford-in-the-Water, there is a turning off the bypass which leads up Kirkdale. A right turn near the top brings one into **Sheldon**, a small village built either side of the main street.

Bakewell

Bakewell is the central town of the Peak and attracts many thousands of visitors. It has interesting groups of buildings and a good selection of shops, both for provisions and souvenirs. Its bookshop carries a wide range of books and papers on the Peak District. Several shops offer Bakewell puddings, preserving the memory of the culinary accident that produced the new dish. The disaster apparently occurred at the Rutland Arms when a maid deputising for the cook was asked to make a strawberry tart. She put the egg mixture on top of the jam instead of (as was usual) into the pastry. The guests were delighted and a local speciality was born.

Although much of Bakewell has been

built since the late nineteenth century, the town centre does have some fine buildings. The **National Park Information Office** is situated in the former Market Hall, which dates from the early seventeenth century. In addition to a very comprehensive collection of local information the Information Centre also houses an interactive exhibition giving a brief overview of the history of the local landscape. Rutland Square – where is now the roundabout – was set out in 1804 when the Rutland Arms was built. This is a fine coaching inn and its stable still remains across the road, the buildings being built around two courtyards, one behind the other.

The **Bath Gardens** adjacent to the Rutland Hotel stables used to be the gardens to Bath House built by the Duke of Rutland in 1697 over a natural spring. Bath House is the last building on the left at the Bath Street end of the gardens and is now occupied by the British Legion. The duke's bath still survives in the cellar and is 33ft (10m) by 16ft (4.8m)! Bakewell failed, however, to develop as a spa town like Buxton and Matlock.

Behind the Rutland Hotel is a small area of old houses, which reward investigation. Just up the road to Monyash (King Street) is the old **Town Hall** on the right, one of the most interesting buildings in the town. It was built in 1602 and housed the Town Hall upstairs and St John's Hospital on the ground floor. Appropriately situated on King Street is the **Bakewell Antiques and Collectors' Centre,** which offers displays of items from dealers from around the country. There is a tea and coffee house on the first floor.

Whilst in that part of town transport enthusiasts might care to visit the **M & C Motorcycle Collection**, just off Matlock Street. British motorcycles from 1900 to the mid 1970s are on display, firstly to celebrate the fine engineering that produced them and secondly to support the Bakewell and Eyam Community Transport venture.

Bakewell has one of the oldest schools in the county – Lady Manners – dating from 1636. The original building was a cottage in South Church Street, behind the old Town Hall. In 1826, it moved to the latter, where the upper floor had been in use as the Court and Quarter Sessions. From 1896 to 1936 it used the Town Hall building in Bath Street and on its 300th anniversary, the foundation stone of the current school in Shutts Lane was laid.

Beyond the Town Hall is **All Saints' Church**, situated on an elevated site with its steeple dominating the skyline. There are two ancient crosses in the churchyard, of the ninth and eleventh centuries. The one beneath the eastern end of the church was found in Two Dales, north of Matlock. Pevsner regards the accumulated headstones and coffin slabs, housed in the south porch, as the largest and most varied group of medieval monuments housed in the United Kingdom. They were found during restoration work in 1841-2. Some of the stones date from the Anglo-Saxon period and these presumably include the scroll work in pieces to the right as one goes through the porch. More of these carved stones can be seen on the west wall of the nave.

The church is well lit and many signs indicate specific items of interest. The

Above: The Bakewell Pudding shop, Bakewell

Above: Haddon Hall, near Bakewell

Above: Bakewell Show

west end is Norman, with two surviving arches in what could be the walls of an earlier Saxon building, now the walls between the nave and the adjacent aisles. Much of the present church was built in the thirteenth century but the spire, octagon and south transept (known as the Newark) had to be taken down and rebuilt in the nineteenth century.

Behind and above the church is the **Old House Museum**, constructed in limestone with a stone flagged roof. It was built in 1543 as a parsonage house, extended in about 1620, and was turned into tenements by Sir Richard Arkwright some 250 years later. Bakewell Historical Society started a restoration scheme in 1959. It now displays its original wattle and daub interior walls in fourteen rooms of fascinating folk history. To the east of the church is Bagshaw Hill, with Bagshaw Hall (built in 1684) half way down on the left.

To complete a circular tour of the town centre, cross the A6 at the bottom of Bagshaw Hill and walk past the Millford Hotel to the mill leat of Victoria Corn Mill (which still has its iron waterwheel in the millyard, having been lifted out of the wheelpit for restoration but now sadly decaying). Turn down-stream and follow the leat to Castle Street which brings you out by the bridge over the River Wye, which was built in 1300. Just a little upstream is Holme Bridge, a packhorse bridge built in 1694 and now a footbridge. There is a sheepwash and interpretation board at the A6-road end of the bridge.

There is a pleasant riverside walk downstream from Castle Street and the bridge. This eventually reaches the park, a large recreation ground with a cricket pitch, football pitch and swings for young children at the far side. If you have your dog with you, this is a pleasant area to exercise it.

Bakewell is a very popular visitor centre and parking is not always easy to find. There are a large number of shops including those selling crafts, aromatherapy oils, books and the daily requirements of a large town. There are two courtyard shopping areas, one in Matlock Street and one in Portland Square (off Water Street) that should not be overlooked. A number of high quality outlets operate in the town, including the **Original Farmers' Market Shop**, which sells produce of a very high standard from local farmers and producers.

Recently there have been big changes in the centre of Bakewell. A new agricultural centre incorporating the cattle market has been built on the east side of the river clearing the way for a new development from the Market Hall area to the river on the west bank. The new project includes shops, housing, a new swimming pool and a supermarket. The cattle market is still held every Monday where visitors can view the auctions taking place and marvel at the speed of the auctioneers.

Bakewell Show, held annually in August, this used to be the largest single day agricultural show in the country but now extends to two days. It is a large event and there are usually many stalls and displays to interest visitors. In addition to craft stalls selling a wide range of quality items there is an enormous marquee with floral displays organised by the Women's Institute.

Additionally, of course, there are the stands for farmers and gardeners and the inevitable beer tent! A visit to the show is recommended, but aim to arrive reasonably early – it is very popular! **Bakewell Arts Festival** runs for a week immediately following the Show offering performing arts, music and street entertainers.

Perhaps the main point of interest of Bakewell is that it acts as a centre for visiting different parts of the Peak and of course the two major houses of the area – Chatsworth and Haddon Hall. The latter lies just down the river from the town and is well worth a visit. It is very much older than Chatsworth, and is claimed by many to be Britain's most complete non-fortified medieval house.

Haddon Hall stands adjacent to the A6, hidden by trees and a beech hedge. The car park is across the road, so that one approaches the gatehouse on foot. The entrance is impressive with two lines of mature beech hedges converging at an old packhorse bridge over the wide but shallow waters of the River Wye. The house itself stands on a bluff overlooking the river and the bridge, although somewhat masked by the trees, and the entrance is at the foot of the north-west tower with a very low doorway.

The battlemented buildings are set around two courtyards paved with flagstones. In the south-west corner of the Hall and lower courtyard is situated the chapel. This is probably the oldest part of the Hall, for parts of the chapel were built by William Peveril around 1080-90. The altar slab in the south aisle of the chapel is of Norman origin as are the two fonts in other parts of the chapel. It has a three-decker pulpit and various pews built by Sir George Manners in 1624. The chapel is very well lit by natural means and remarkably well preserved. It contrasts greatly with the chapel of Chatsworth, which is resplendent in all its richness.

The old kitchens on the left of the entrance to the banqueting hall still retain such items as bowls carved into the wooden bench tops. Beyond the kitchen is the bakehouse and butcher's shop, which provided essential food for the house. The entrance hall opens into the banqueting hall which was built around 1350 by Sir Richard Vernon, and this is essentially as he built it with oak panelling and a large open fireplace. The minstrel's gallery was added later, however. The long table in the hall is 400 years old and contrasts with the roof above it, which had to be replaced in 1924. Even so the new roof is a genuine attempt to recreate the style of the old. Leading off the banqueting hall is the dining room dating from 1500, which was added by Sir Henry Vernon. This is a delightful room with much carved panelling showing the coat-of-arms of the Talbot family, and Edward VI when Prince of Wales.

Above the dining room on the first floor is the great chamber with a remarkable number of tapestries plus moulded plasterwork. In a succession of rooms the visitor notes advise of architectural details dating parts of the building to around 1500 or even earlier. Haddon Hall is an amazing survival, in a very good state of repair, of this period of English architecture. The long gallery with its heraldic glass window dated 1589, beautifully carved stone mullions, and panelled walls carved as long ago as the middle of the sixteenth century make this one of the most beautiful rooms in the house. The room also has a delightful painting by Rex Whistler, painted before his famous mural at Plas Newydd on Anglesey. It shows the house, the Duke of Rutland (who restored the house) and his son, the late duke.

In the latter half of the seventeenth century the Duke of Rutland moved his family seat to Belvoir Castle in Leicestershire, so that for well over 200 years the Hall became more or less empty and unused, although still maintained. This is the reason why the Hall was never 'restored' or rebuilt.

The garden at Haddon is always a delight in the summer, especially when the roses and clematis are in bloom. It consists of six large terraces, although unfortunately the upper ones are not open to the public. Judged the 'Garden of the Year' by Christies and the Historic Houses Association recently, this garden really does justify its reputation.

There is a first floor self-service restaurant in the old stable block as you approach the Hall and a gift shop in the Gate House. A Regular Visitor's pass is available for those visiting several times during the year. The car park is 400 yards (366m) from the hall. Parking closer than this may be available for the disabled but access to the house is difficult for those with limited mobility, due to the many steps and uneven surfaces.

Just below Haddon lies **Rowsley**. Here the Lathkill joins the Wye at Picory Corner and the combined waters flow towards the Derwent. A small village, Rowsley used to boast a substantial railway marshalling yard – a relic of the days when Rowsley was the rail head of the Midland Railway's line from Derby and prior to the building of the connection with Buxton which began in 1860. Now it is very different. A shopping outlet centre, **Peak Village**, has been created on the site, of the old station building that was designed by Joseph Paxton and opened in 1849. There is a restaurant/coffee shop and a fitness centre.

Rowsley boasts a very fine hotel, the **Peacock**, originally built in 1652, which later became a dower house of Haddon Hall. If you fancy dinner, or an overnight stay in one of the Peacock Hotel's four-poster beds, this upmarket hotel is for you. It also has seven miles (11.2km) of fishing on the River Wye and two miles (3.2km) on the River Derwent available for residents.

At Rowsley, the River Wye joins the Derwent, flowing south from the northern gritstone moors past Calver and Chatsworth. Rowsley also has a working museum at **Caudwell's Mill**. Built in 1875, the mill was originally driven by waterwheels. These were replaced by turbines, which still power the machinery.

Visitors can see flour being made, purchase flour (including speciality flours such as pastry flour and French flour for crusty rolls) or enjoy refreshments in the tea room. There is also a craft centre and gallery to augment the income of the voluntary trust which rescued and runs the mill.

Another group of volunteers has also commenced work in Rowsley;

The Peacock, Rowsley

Of particular interest to residents and visitors is a ceramic peacock just inside the entrance. It is one of five made by Minton of Stoke-on-Tent in 1850-1, and this one went down with the ship *Loch Ard* in 1878, 14 miles (22.4km) off Moonlight Heads, Victoria, Australia. It was brought up during salvage operations, and eventually came back to England. Minton traced four of their peacocks and a visitor from Australia told the hotel that she had number five, also brought up from the hapless *Loch Ard*.

Peak Rail have been excavated the site of Rowsley Shed, uncovering the old brick floors and inspection pits. They have restored the line to Rowsley from Matlock and it is possible to arrive here on a train again (see chapter 3). The Society wishes to re-establish the rail link with Buxton, but a major obstacle is the need for a new bridge across the A6 at this point. With considerable congestion in Bakewell – almost a daily feature in summer – a park and ride scheme using the railway seems to have a lot of merit.

The River Derwent can be followed upstream to Chatsworth Park where there is a convenient free car park at Calton Lees, which can be used to visit the **Chatsworth Garden Centre**, or to walk to Chatsworth through the park and alongside the river. Alternatively there is a car park at the house itself. Chatsworth is described in Chapter 6.

North of the Wye

The limestone region north of the River Wye is a patchwork of small villages and undulating farmland cut by deep valleys such as Cressbrook Dale, Coombs Dale and Middleton Dale. To the east it is overlooked by Longstone Edge, with the scar of High Rake Mine. The latter was once the scene of the worst financial lead mining venture

Foolow

in the whole of the Peak. It is now an opencast site, worked more recently for fluorspar rather than lead ore.

Apart from Eyam, which is situated on the edge of the gritstone and is reserved for a later chapter, the largest village is **Tideswell**. There must be many visitors to the Peak who miss – or drive straight through – Tideswell. With its multitude of shops – including a Co-op, a chemist, two restaurants, bank, post office and filling station – it can satisfy most requirements of a visitor. For the twenty-first century it has a touch screen kiosk at the main bus stop, allowing residents and visitors alike to access local information and history.

The area around the church is a pure gem. Park near the **church of St John the Baptist** and have a look at the George Hotel, a fine coaching inn with Venetian windows and dating from 1730. To the rear of the church is the vicarage and at its side, the library, a superb example of vernacular architecture combining cut blocks of limestone with gritstone quoins and mullions.

Fortunately for visitors, a leaflet gives a concise history of the church for there is much to see. There is a wealth of different brasses, some very old, including one showing Bishop Pursglove of Hull, who was a native of Tideswell, in full eucharistic vestments as worn before the Reformation. The original church was enlarged in the fourteenth century and is very impressive. It took so long to build that the architectural style started off at the east end in Early English style. By the time the masons were building the west end, the Perpendicular was in fashion and it was in this style that the building was finished. It certainly

should be visited, and fully lives up to its title of 'Cathedral of the Peak'.

Elsewhere the villages follow the familiar pattern, either elongated or set around a village square. Most are very small but with little features here and there that make a visit worthwhile such as the stocks in **Litton**; the fourteenth-century cross and adjacent village pond in Foolow; and the memorial to James Brindley, the canal engineer, at **Wormhill**, where he was born.

East of Litton on the road to Wardlow Mires is the top of Cressbrook Dale, its steep-sided valley coming right up to the road. A pronounced feature of this end of the valley is **Peter's Stone**, which is a detached block of limestone of significant size. It can be viewed from the A623 at Wardlow Mires, but the sign-posted footpath from there down the top of the dale enables you to get quite close.

Mention of the fourteenth-century cross in **Foolow** has been made above. It is worth more than a passing glance. The cross was resited on the green in 1868 at the rear of a flat stone with an iron ring set in its top surface. The stone is a bull baiting stone and must be very old, for bull baiting was made illegal in 1835. The cross stands by the old village mere, fed by a spring with a wall around it. Around this centre sit the village school, manor house, pub, chapel and other old village buildings dating from the seventeenth and eighteenth centuries.

Half a mile (800m) along the road to Eyam is Waterfall Farm, on the right hand side. It takes its name from an unusual waterfall. A small stream rising on the side of Eyam Edge flows down to a swallet hole just beyond the farm. Here the water drops some 20ft (6m) before disappearing into broken rock.

Places to Visit

℗ Parking Available
♿ Disabled Facilities
👪 Family Attraction
<№ Concession for under certain ages
☂ Suitable in Wet Weather

Buxton

Pump Room
The Crescent
Open: April to end of September.
Exhibition of local arts and crafts.

Buxton Opera House
Water Street
☎ 0845 12 72190
www.buxton-opera.co.uk
Open: all year.
Productions ranging from drama to comedy, opera to children's shows, musical theatre to one-man shows.

Buxton Museum and Art Gallery
Terrace Road SK17 6DA
☎ 01298 24658
Open: 9.30am–5.30pm, Tue– Fri and 9.30am–5pm on Sat, all year. Also 10.30am–5pm on Sun and Bank Holidays from Easter to end of Sep.
Award winning 'Wonders of the Peak' journeying through time from 'Big Bang' to the Victorians. Extensive collections of geology, archaeology, prehistory and local history. Special exhibitions and events.
℗ Nearby ♿ 👪 <15 ☂

Poole's Cavern and Country Park
Green Lane SK17 9DH
☎ 01298 26978
www.poolescavern.co.uk
Open: 9.30am-5pm daily, Mar–end-Oct. Some winter opening but closed Tues in term time and weekends in Nov.
Spectacular natural limestone cavern, woodland trail, Solomon's Temple, picnic area.

Go Ape! High Wire Forest Adventure
Green Lane
☎ 0870 220 4792
www.goape.co.uk
Open: Daily end Mar–end Oct. Weekends only Nov. 9am-dusk. Pre-booking essential.

Buxton Raceway
Dalehead Rd. Off A53 Buxton to Leek Road
☎ 01663 741353, race days only 01663 741353
www.buxtonraceway.com
Open: meetings on many Sun and Bank Holidays from Mar–end-Oct.
Banger racing including championship qualifying races.
℗ ♿ 👪9-15 ☂

Around Buxton

Dunge Valley Hidden Gardens
Kettleshulme SK23 7RF
☎ 01663 733787
www.dungevalley.co.uk
Open: 10.30am-5pm, Mar–Jun, Thu–Sun and Bank Holiday Mondays.
Beautiful valley garden specialising in rhododendrons, acers and magnolias. Good scent for the blind. Hardy plant nursery. Tea room.
Bakewell
℗ 👪<16

Places to Visit

Bakewell

Bakewell Antiques and Collector's Centre

King Street
☎ 01629 812496
Open: 10am-5pm Mon–Sat, 12.30-5pm Sun.

M & C Collection of Historic Motorcycles

Off Matlock Street DE45 1EF
☎ 01629 815011
www.mccollection.net
Open: 11am–5pm on certain weekends over the summer. Telephone for details. Basic motorcycles, to tourers, scramble bikes, and racing machines.
Ⓟmotorcycles only ♿ ⋔<16, 7-16 ☎

Old House Museum

Cunningham Place, Off Church Lane DE45 1DD
☎ 01629 813642
Open: 11–4pm daily, Apr–end-Oct
Parties booked for morning or evening visits. Folk Museum in historic early sixteenth-century house, once owned by Sir Richard Arkwright and partitioned to house some of his workforce.

South of Bakewell

Haddon Hall

Bakewell DE45 1LA
Two miles (3.25km) south of Bakwell on A6
☎ 01629 812855
www.haddonhall.co.uk
Open: noon-5pm daily May–Sep. Apr and Oct, Sat–Mon
Medieval and Tudor manor house with magnificent terraced rose garden, set in the beautiful valley of the River Wye.
Ⓟnearby ⋔<5 ☎other than long path from carpark

Caudwell's Mill and Craft Centre

Bakewell Rd, Rowsley, Matlock DE4 2EB
☎ 01629 734374 (mill)
or 733185 (craft centre)
Open: mill – 10am–6pm daily Apl–Oct; winter: 10am–4.30pm.
Craft shop open daily all year.
Historic water-powered flour mill, café, gift shop, working crafts including wood turner, glass blower, artist, and jewellery gallery. Wholemeal flour always available.
Guided tours by arrangement (including evenings) in summer.

5. The Dark Peak and Eyam

Eyam Hall

North of the limestone region lies the Dark Peak. Strictly speaking the Dark Peak includes the area of the Upper Derwent Valley and the moors east of there, but for convenience these have been included in Chapter 6. It is really an unfortunate description, for it connotes a forbidding area, and although there are areas of desolate moorland, much of it is not. The gritstone regions that surround the limestone include some of the best scenery in the Peak District. In fact, many will find the Dark Peak of more interest than the limestone district further south. In addition to the great expanse of peat moors such as Kinder Scout and Bleaklow there are the less rigorous walking areas of the Hope and Edale valleys, separated by the ridge between Lose Hill and Mam Tor, with the isolated Win Hill situated at the end of the Hope valley and blocking the east-west trend of the Edale valley. Here can be seen some of the best countryside that the Peak has to offer.

To the south lies Bradwell, at the neck of a valley between the somewhat featureless Bradwell Moor and Bradwell Edge where the gritstones drop steeply to the limestones and the White Peak.

Background

This is an area of significant historical interest. The Iron Age hillfort on Mam Tor commands an impressive position and sits astride a routeway possibly as old as the earliest colonisation of the Peak. Later the Romans established a fort at *Navio*, near Brough, north-west of Bradwell. Their roads stretched away to Buxton, along Doctor's Gate to *Ardotalia* and eastwards towards Sheffield. Relics of their occupation can be seen in Buxton Museum. Later, a Norman castle was built nearby, giving its name to the settlement below it – Castleton. The keep still survives, together with much of its perimeter wall. All around are the relics of the once important lead mining industry and hundreds of shafts pockmark the landscape. Beneath Mam Tor is the Odin Mine, traditionally said to have been worked by the Saxons. There is no evidence to prove this, but it all helps to create the impression of antiquity in the area.

Further Roman roads can be traced in this area such as the road from *Aquae Arnemetiae* to *Ardotalia* (Buxton to Glossop) and a good account of them is given in *Peakland Roads and Trackways* by AE and EM Dodd. Of more recent origin are the numerous packhorse routes which cross the area, many making useful footpaths, such as the Edale to Castleton path via Hollins Cross which can be traced on the OS map in its entirety. Alternatively, north-west of Hope Cross, the Roman road which is now a bridle path crosses Blackley Clough where other hollow ways can be seen, now completely disused, but worn down over centuries

of use. The legacy of these old roadways is an important network of paths, which enable us to explore the area.

Of equal interest are the remains of early settlements. There is little to see at the Roman forts of *Navio* at Brough and *Ardotalia* at Glossop. However, it is possible to walk around what remains of the latter. It is a rectangular site and the stone foundations have been excavated. Looking around it is clear just how commanding a position it occupied.

Mam Tor's Iron Age fort, apparently built around the fifth century BC, is more interesting. Its dominating position above the impregnable south-facing cliff of Mam Tor is impressive in itself, with magnificent views down the valleys. For the curious, however, the ramparts remain except where the vertical cliff facing Castleton has eaten into the hillside. You can park close to the fort at the car park on the Chapel-en-le-Frith-Castleton road at Rushup Edge (SK124833). Mam Tor and the Winnats form part of the National Trust's 30,000 acre (12,000 hectare) High Peak Estate, which also includes much of the Dark Peak.

Below Mam Tor sits Castleton, on an outpost of limestone worked for centuries for lead, Blue John stone and now for cement. Above the village is **Peveril Castle** on a site reminiscent of Mam Tor fort with its sheer drop to Cave Dale and protected flank. The most impressive view of the castle keep, looking across the dry valley, is from Cave Dale. The alternative view, of course, is from the village below.

The castle was built in 1080 by William Peveril, the illegitimate son of William the Conqueror, as a wooden stockade. This was later rebuilt in stone and the stone keep was added in 1175. The castle was only one of several in the Peak, others existing at Bakewell, Ashford-in-the-Water, Hathersage and Pilsbury, north of Hartington, but these were minor affairs; Peveril Castle was by far the most important. It seems to have been a hunting lodge of the Royal Forest of the High Peak and Henry II happened to be here when he received the submission of King Malcolm of Scotland in 1157. The climb up to the castle (owned by English Heritage) looks daunting but it is fairly easy if you are fit. The perimeter wall survives largely complete and the site of various internal buildings can be seen. The keep can be entered, but there is not a lot to see inside.

Doctor's Gate

On the moors, the early lines of communication have remained relatively intact, especially the possible Roman road known as Doctor's Gate. Whatever its age, this narrow track is an amazing relic and a watchful eye needs to be kept to ensure its preservation. The track is actually named after Dr John Talbot, an illegitimate son of the Earl of Shrewsbury, who was the vicar of Glossop from 1494 until 1550. Presumably he would have used the road when travelling from his home to his father's castle at Sheffield. The track is 3-5ft (1-1.5m) wide and can be seen to advantage on Coldharbour Moor, where the original paving slabs and kerbstones are intact.

The Plague Village

Eyam is another village steeped in history and interest. It is a small and attractive village nestling under Eyam Edge with several interesting streets and some fine properties. It is perhaps most well known for the tenacity of its villagers when stricken by the plague in 1665. The story is well documented elsewhere but, briefly, the disease reached the village in a consignment of cloth sent from London. Encouraged by their vicar, the villagers decided to cut themselves off from the outside world and although the disease abated during the cold winter months, it returned with ferocious consequences in the summer of 1666. In all a total of 257 villagers died. The full story is told in **Eyam Museum.**

Today, the Plague Cottage where it all started can be seen on the main road just west of the church. Close to Plague Cottage it is ironic to read a notice stating that the village has one of the oldest communal water supplies in the country. The grassy area to the left of the cottages is the site of the old village pond and the nearby village stocks still survive in front of the hall, which dates from the seventeenth century. **Eyam Hall** is now open to the public. The house was built fifty years after the plague and is worthy of a visit. In the farmyard are a buttery, gift shop and craft centre, where amongst others is a maker of stringed instruments.

In the churchyard are graves to the plague victims including Catherine Mompesson, the wife of the vicar. William Mompesson acted as leader, comforter and liaison officer with the

A walk around Abney and Eyam Moor

This moorland area has some excellent footpaths. A good circular route of about 10 miles (16km) gives a good impression of the area. Foolow makes a convenient starting point.

Take the Bretton road out of the village for about half a mile (800m) and then take the path to Abney Grange, first ascending Eyam Edge. Descend into Bretton Clough to cross the Bretton Brook and climb up to Abney Grange. Turn west at the grange and upon reaching the Hucklow Edge to Abney road, cross the road and Abney Moor to the junction of two lanes near Robin Hood's Cross, of which only the base remains. It is probably a boundary cross, although it is also at the crossing of packhorse routes from Brough and Bradwell. At the junction bear right and proceed north-east along Shatton Lane around Shatton Edge. Descend some distance towards Shatton village before taking a path off to the right which leads roughly eastwards towards Offerton Hall. It nestles under Offerton Moor overlooking Hathersage with a fine view towards the moors which separate the Derwent Valley from Sheffield.

From Offerton Hall take the track to Highlow Hall around Offerton Moor and dropping down into the wooded Dunge Brook. From here take the Abney Road and opposite the drive to The Oaks drop down into the valley of Highlow Brook to Stoke Ford.

Here Abney Clough meets Bretton Clough and the path crosses a footbridge and climbs up the east side of Bretton Clough. A well-defined track crosses Eyam Moor heading for Mag Clough where it reaches the road across Sir William Hill from Great Hucklow to Grindleford. From here take the Eyam road, which passes Mompesson's Well.

Pass the youth hostel at Beech Hurst and descend the road into the village. From Eyam there is a choice of routes back to Foolow. Either take the road, or the path through the fields just to the south of the road, which is more pleasant and slightly more direct.

If the climb out of Foolow up the side of Eyam Edge is too strenuous, start from the top of Eyam Edge and ignore Eyam village by turning right upon reaching the road across Sir William Hill.

Eyam Church and cross

outside world but was not spared the life of his wife. She lies buried near to the village cross. This Celtic cross should not be missed. Although not complete, it is a remarkable survivor, perhaps all the more striking because the cross head survives on top of the shaft together with its intricate carving.

Beyond the church one can find graves of plague victims who were buried in makeshift graves, perhaps to maintain family isolation, or when the graveyard reached its capacity. It makes one wonder how many lie in unmarked resting places beyond the churchyard wall. Look for the seven Hancock graves east of the village at **Riley House Farm**. Follow the main road out of the village to the east, past the old chapel to Riley Wood, where there is a lane on the left. This lane brings you to the walled enclosure where the family lie buried. It is about half a mile (800m) or so out of the village. Church services were held in the open during the time of the plague at **Cucklet Delf** and a service of remembrance is held there annually.

The Hathersage road rises up past Eyam Youth Hostel and continues climbing around a sharp bend to the left. There is a left turn to Bretton, which should be ignored, and after a few more yards, **Mompesson's Well** may be seen on the left. It is protected by railings and is where the villagers left money for goods during the plague. What a terrible ordeal that must have been, especially when some villagers could possibly have been saved if they had fled rather than isolated themselves.

One of our nursery rhymes has a

special significance to Eyam:

> Ring a ring of roses,
> A pocket full of posies,
> Atishoo, Atishoo,
> We all fall down.

The ring of roses – a rash on the chest – was the first sign of the plague; the posies relate to fragrant flowers used to cover the smell of the infection, and the sneezing signalled the final stage of the illness prior to death.

Eyam Edge affords some good panoramic views marred perhaps by the fluorspar treatment plant of Laporte Industries at Cavendish Mill situated across Middleton Dale. It is nonetheless a salutary reminder that these beautiful places also have to sustain work to maintain the fabric of the area, whether or not we like the consequences. It comes as no surprise that from time to time the planning authority comes into conflict with industry; quarrying and mining operations present a continual problem in this conservation-conscious era. Laporte Industries process a very fine quality fluorspar from Sallet Hole Mine on Longstone Edge and from opencast workings, plus spar from other 'tributors' in the area.

Behind Eyam village, the ground rises to **Eyam Moor**, with its numerous cairns and stone circle. This high ground stretches northwards towards the Hope and Derwent Valleys and westwards to Great Hucklow where it is known as **Abney Moor**. The Bretton Brook cuts a big slice out of the moor and it drains the area to the north-east. The whole area is like a huge island of about 10 sq miles (26 sq km) surrounded by edges and steeply descending ground. It is an area often neglected by tourists, yet the Great Hucklow to Hathersage road cuts right across the area.

There are some good views across Eyam Moor from the road – which runs past the **Derbyshire & Lancashire Gliding Club** at Camphill farm – through the tiny village of Abney and also past **Highlow Hall**. The latter is not a contradiction in terms in the Peak, for 'low' is a very common Derbyshire word meaning burial mound or burial hill. The Hall was the home of the Eyre family and is one of several sixteenth-century houses in the area. Offerton Hall to the north-west and Hazlebadge Hall south of Bradwell are other examples.

Castleton and its Caves

There is much to commend **Castleton** and it is easy to spend a day in the area. Even in poor weather, it is possible to avoid the rain by going underground in one of the four show caves or by visiting the various shops, the church, information centre and museum (the Ollerenshaw Collection) in the village. Let us start however with the caves.

Only one is a true cave – **Peak Cavern**, which is owned by the Duchy of Lancaster. It used to be known as the 'Devil's Arse in the Peak' but such vulgarity did not survive Victorian sensitivity. The cave system is very extensive, far more so than the portion open to the visitor. From its mouth flows the Peakshole Water, which originates as a number of streams flowing off the moor above. The cave entrance was used for making ropes and the rope walk can still be seen. Gone, however, are the little ropemakers' cottages that used to stand within the entrance to the cave itself. Ropes have been made here for centuries and Castleton brides used to be presented with a locally-made washing line.

Three more show caves, or more strictly speaking, mines with natural caves in them, exist at Treak Cliff below Mam Tor. On Treak Cliff itself are **Blue John Mine** and **Treak Cliff Cavern.** The former is a mine for Blue John stone, much favoured by the Victorians for decoration.

The purplish stone is a variety of fluorspar that has been impregnated with hydrocarbons. The main veins, now fully exploited, were used to create beautiful vases and inlay work. Chatsworth has one of the largest vases turned from a single piece of stone and Kedleston Hall near to Derby has much Blue John inlay work. There is a good display of the stone, both in turned work and in cross sections, in Buxton Museum. Nowadays only a few hundredweight a year are mined, for costume jewellery. The age of the workings is unknown but it is unlikely to be more than two to three hundred years.

Blue John Mine descends steeply with countless steps to the bottom, which can be slippery in wet weather so ensure you wear suitable footwear. Treak Cliff Cavern includes some rather fine grottoes of stalactites and stalagmites, which were discovered during a search for fresh veins of Blue John stone in 1926. Several veins of Blue John stone may be seen, together with the

The Dark Peak and Eyam

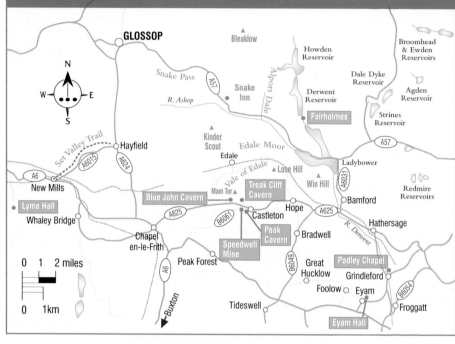

largest piece ever found which weighs about 16 tons. There is a café and picnic area where you can eat your own food. This mine is easy to walk through. It has a gift shop selling Blue John ornaments and jewellery.

The **Speedwell Mine**, actually across the Winnats Pass from Treak Cliff, is advertised as being a unique experience – the only mine where visitors are conducted underground by boat. The mine was designed like this in 1774. The popularity of Castleton means that during the summer, you may find parking difficult and queues at the caves.

The adjacent **Winnats Pass** is spectacular. It is thought to have been eroded when it was under the sea rather than being a former cave system. It is

Above: The head of the Hope Valley from near the Blue John Cavern

Blue John Cavern

Peak Cavern

Treak Cliff Cavern

Speedwell Mine

The Castleton garland ceremony

This attracts a lot of interest on the evening of 29 May when the Garland King and his lady proceed on horseback through the village. The king carries a 60lb (27kg) frame around him which is decked with flowers. The procession stops at each of the six inns in the village and eventually the garland is hoisted to hang from one of the pinnacles of the church tower, after the top bunch of flowers has been formally placed on the war memorial. It is pleasant to witness such ancient ceremonies surviving in our modern age.

only open to cars and light traffic, but whether on foot, car or bike it is worth seeing. It used to be the main turnpike road until the latter was re-routed under Mam Tor because the gradient was easier. Unfortunately the face of Mam Tor is continually eroding due to hard bands of gritstone lying on softer shale. This has given rise to the name 'Shivering Mountain' but sometimes the movement is more severe, resulting in landslips that affect the road, causing subsidence on a large scale. The road is now permanently closed and has been abandoned completely. Meanwhile although cars can use the Winnats Pass road, it should be negotiated with care, especially when it is icy. Heavy traffic must divert via Bradwell and Peak Forest.

Under Treak Cliff is the Odin Mine, which was worked for lead and not Blue John. Although its name implies a Saxon connection, there is no evidence of it being worked prior to the seventeenth century. Its main interest to the visitor is the crushing circle, which survives on the east side of the road just above the Treak Cliff Cavern. The main entrance to the mine was lost during road-widening operations and although the large opening west of the road does lead into the workings, **these are dangerous and should not be entered**.

The crushing circle consists of a cast-iron track upon which lead ore would be heaped. This was then crushed by the millstone (5ft 10in (1.8m) diameter) which would be rolled around a pivot by a horse. The millstone with its circular iron tyre also survives, and it is an interesting relic of this bygone era and industry. The old mine tips are also a useful place to get out of the car and photograph the upper end of the Hope Valley and Castleton village itself.

If you do not feel energetic enough to visit the caves you can see the products of Blue John in the village gift shops. The information centre has a display on lead mining, while a few yards away is the old hall (now a youth hostel). The adjacent vicarage has also been acquired by the Youth Hostels Association and converted into seven ensuite rooms. Additionally, a former barn at the rear has been converted into two separate suites. All are available for hire on a room basis by families and individuals.

Opposite is St Edmund's church, noted for its collection of old bibles, some of which are on display. This is a lovely small church with interesting

Multi-activity holidays

Other accommodation is available at the Edale Youth Hostel Activity Centre. This is one of the country's leading licensed centres for activity-based holidays. Courses are run on abseiling, archery, caving, climbing, canoeing, hang-gliding, kayaking, mountain biking, navigation, orienteering, pony trekking or walking. Courses can be for the weekend or for longer periods. Accommodation is available in private rooms or in traditional dormitories. Two rooms have ensuite facilities.

box pews and a magnificent Norman archway.

In contrast to the caves of Castleton would be a visit to the conservation park of the **Chestnut Centre** about 6 miles (10km) to the west of Castleton via Winnats Pass. Otters and owls are the speciality here with extensive breeding programmes designed to allow release into the wild to supplement diminishing numbers.

Bradwell to Edale

Before leaving this area for the Edale Valley one must not forget **Bradwell**, at the north end of Bradwell Dale. It grew as a mining community and it retains that character. Bradwell used to be famous for the hard hats made there, which the miners used and which were known as 'Bradder Beavers'.

Nearby is the village of **Hope**. Its ancient church has a fourteenth-century broach-spire which is unusual in the Peak District. The rest of the church is much later, but there are one or two interesting features such as a Saxon cross shaft in the churchyard and two fonts, one of the twelfth century and another of 1662 which was brought from Derwent church when the latter was demolished to make way for Lady-bower Reservoir.

Dominating the landscape behind the village are the twin hills of Lose Hill and Win Hill. Between the two hills flows the River Noe to join the Peakshole Water at Hope village. This narrow valley carries the river together with the road and railway line to Edale. After 2 or 3 miles (3-5km) the valley turns westwards and opens out considerably. Here is the Vale of Edale in which the tiny village of Edale nestles under Kinder Scout. The peacefulness of this little valley is often ruptured in summer, but the tranquility returns in winter, particularly under a blanket of snow.

To the south of the valley is the ridge from Lose Hill via Mam Tor to Lord's Seat on Rushup Edge. Along the ridge runs a footpath, which is an old pack-horse route from Chapel-en-le-Frith via Mam Tor and Hollins Cross to Hope and onwards through Hathersage to Sheffield. Today this is a marvellous footpath which can be used as part of a 7 mile (11.2km) circular route based on Castleton.

From the Market Place in Castleton, take the path up Cave Dale to where it reaches an old green lane between Dirtlow Rake and Eldon Hill. Bear north-west along the old Portway

121

The Keep, Peveril Castle

Castleton Garland ceremony

Cottages, Edale

Lose Hill

which heads for Mam Tor hill fort. From here take the ridge towards Lose Hill passing Hollins Cross and Back Tor; return to Castleton via the public right of way that runs from Lose Hill Farm via Riding House Farm and skirts the western side of Losehill Hall. Several old packhorse routes, now footpaths, meet at Hollins Cross.

Indeed it used to be the main road between Castleton and Edale and stories are still recalled of mill girls working in Edale who used to live in Castleton and walk this way to work, often having to spend the night at the mill when inclement weather prevented their return in the winter.

Losehill Hall is now a residential centre run by the National Park, where weekly courses are organised, covering many aspects of activities in the Peak District. Whether your interest is history, botany, geology, the history of old mines, caves, railways or industrial archaeology of the area, all these interests and many more are catered for here.

A look on the map at the ground south of Rushup Edge shows various small streams that flow off the edge and suddenly disappear. These streams flow into a complex of underground passages, which include Giant's Hole and the very wet cave well-known in caving circles as P8. They reappear in Peak Cavern and the other caves at Castleton. Giant's Hole lives up to its name for it is almost 500ft (154m) deep and a large system of passages leads out from its base.

Just to the south of Giant's Hole is Eldon Hole where the main entrance shaft is almost 200ft (61.5m)

deep. Needless to say there are many other smaller cave systems and this particular area is very popular with cavers. Unfortunately many of the caves are watercourses and occasional cave rescue operations have to be mounted here. Eldon Hole can be seen from the A623 east of Peak Forest, where there is the pronounced 'dog-leg' in the road. Alternatively, it may be viewed from the footpath at the end of the lane that runs eastwards from the end of Eldon Lane, near Peak Forest village. The hole may be seen on the north side of the path.

Edale is not a large village but it attracts thousands of visitors both during the summer months and in the winter when it is popular with skiers. The village inn, the Nag's Head, was the first ranger post in the Peak Park, established by the late Tom Tomlinson. From the initial beginnings, the highly professional team of rangers developed. The Rambler Inn, near to the railway station, is now owned by the Ramblers Association and is a pub and guest house. Older visitors to Edale may remember this as the Church Inn. There is a little tearoom nearby on the station approach.

Edale also marks the beginning of the Pennine Way and many ramblers can be seen climbing the path up Grindsbrook. This is a delightful route with many interesting views back towards the village and over to Hollins Cross and Back Tor. The path leads up onto Kinder Scout and it is amazing just how many people head ill-prepared for this area. Kinder Scout, Bleaklow and Saddleworth Moor beyond should not be treated lightly, even in the summer. What can be a sunny pleasant day down in the valleys can turn into a nightmare with the descent of thick fog and mist up on the open moors and peat hags. It is not without good reason that Edale has a mountain rescue post and information centre. There are also three National Trust Information Barns in the Edale Valley.

Just below the turn for Edale Youth Hostel at Nether Booth, there is a good path that starts at Clough Farm and climbs slowly up past Jagger's Clough (a jagger man was in charge of a packhorse team) to Hope Cross and the tree line above Ladybower Reservoir. To your right at this point will be Win Hill, with the whole of the Edale Valley behind you. In fact in all directions the views are memorable.

The Cross (with a capstone dated 1737) is on a Roman road. A path drops down from this into the valley or you can head more directly to Edale End Farm, before returning up the road to Clough Farm. Although an Ordnance Survey map is recommended, it ought to be fairly easy to do these three walks without one.

If you are looking for a more leisurely stroll in the Edale Valley, you can walk up Grindsbrook (behind the Nag's Head Inn), until you reach the steeper climb up onto Kinder Scout; alternatively walk westwards to Upper Booth and onto Jacob's Ladder (this is on the alternative Pennine Way and is fairly flat up to Jacob's Ladder), where the old medieval road rises up to Edale Cross. The latter is dated 1810, the date of its restoration.

Access Land in the National Park

In the 1930s there was much pressure to allow free access to large areas of moorland, contrary to the wishes of the landowners. This culminated in a mass trespass in 1932, when several hundred people left Hayfield village to climb up onto Kinder Scout. Despite the fact that the leaders were jailed after a show trial in Derby (one might even go so far as to say a staged trial) this was only the beginning. It was followed by other mass trespasses, political intrigue, double dealing and eventually the 1949 Act which paved the way for the access agreements which now exist.

The Peak District National Park was founded as a result of the National Parks and Access to the Countryside Act of 1949, which gave the National Park the authority to negotiate agreements with local landowners to permit access to open moorland, irrespective of whether or not rights of way across the land exist.

Access to the moors only exists where a right of way crosses the boundary of land classified as open land. The Dark Peak Ordnance Survey Map shows the boundary of open land and the points of access, but does not cover the eastern moors. On access land one can wander freely, apart from on certain days in the grouse shooting season, between 12 August and 10 December, when parts of the moors are closed. Notices are placed in villages, on railway stations and at access points around the moors giving details.

There are many miles of access land available for public use, most of it in

Mam Tor (foreground) and the ridge to Lose Hill

Edale and Kinder Scout

Moorland Visitor Centre, Edale

The Old Nag's Head Inn, Edale

Win Hill and the Edale Valley from Kinder Scout

the north of the Peak District National Park, but some also on the eastern moors. The public can wander at will on access land, although no damage must be done and it is recommended that you keep to obvious paths, both for your own safety and to avoid unnecessary erosion.

Kinder Scout and Bleaklow

For those wishing to see the northern moors in a less strenuous manner there are two roads that cut through them. The northern one is the A628, the Woodhead road which heads towards Crowden from the Flouch Inn. On the western side of the watershed the valley becomes a long series of reservoirs built for Manchester Corporation. At the top is the oldest, Woodhead, followed by Torside, Rhodeswood, Valehouse and lastly Bottoms Reservoir, almost on the outskirts of Tintwistle village.

Following the closure of the former main railway line between Sheffield and Manchester, the old track has been converted into a footpath called the **Longdendale Trail**, which, in turn, has been incorporated into the Trans Pennine Trail. By using the trail and adjacent access land it is possible to plan excursions up onto the northern side of Kinder Scout or onto Bleaklow. However the reservoirs restrict the number of places where the valley may be crossed to reach Bleaklow. These valleys are wonderful areas to walk in good weather for those properly equipped.

The more southerly route is the A57

road from Glossop to Sheffield. It is more commonly known as the Snake Road and both this and the Woodhead road feature regularly in winter road bulletins as the announcer advises listeners that the roads are blocked by snow. Part of this road is the old Roman road from Brough to Glossop, and as earlier indicated in this chapter, parts of the old road can be seen on Doctor's Gate just to the north of this road, on Coldharbour Moor.

Today's traveller can, however, obtain better comfort than his predecessors because the Duke of Devonshire built an inn, now known as the Snake Pass Inn, in Ladyclough. If you do feel like doing a short walk without experiencing the rigours of the open moors, why not take the footpath up Alport Dale to have a look at **Alport Castles**. This is not some medieval fortification but a natural outcrop, in front of which is a large isolated mass of rock that became separated from the outcrop as a result of a landslip. Alport Castles are situated to the east of Alport Castles Farm, which is about a mile (1.6km) up the dale from the main road at Alport Bridge.

Alport Dale is roughly 4 miles (6.4km) from the end of Ashopton viaduct. In fact there is a milestone at the end of the dale. Parking is not easy however, especially if the available road verge spaces have been taken. The large barn at Alport Castles Farm was first used for Nonconformist worship in 1662. Today this is commemorated with an annual 'Love Feast', which is held here on the first Sunday in July (☎ 01433 650305).

Further up the A57 and beyond the Snake Pass Inn, a bend in the road has been bypassed, making a small car park. If you park here and cross the road to enter the wood, a path drops to the river and follows it for a short distance downstream to where the river reaches a confluence with the stream emerging from Ashop Clough. There is a footbridge here which gives access to the path up the clough. This is a lovely walk and it can be used, like the path up to Alport Castles mentioned above, as a suitable route up onto the moors.

To the west of the moors lie the towns of Glossop and Hayfield, which are joined by the A624. To the west of this road rises Coombes Edge, which marks the western boundary of the Peak District at this point. The boundary of the Peak Park skirts around two towns that developed as textile towns in the nineteenth century. **Glossop** is the larger and has some interesting old buildings, particularly around the town centre and in old Glossop to the east of the town.

Hayfield, however, is a useful starting point for walking up onto the western edge of Kinder Scout and in particular for a walk to **Kinder Downfall**. The Downfall is a waterfall where the River Kinder flows off the edge of Kinder Scout. It is particularly well known for blowing back with the force of the wind, and quite often it freezes up during the harshness of the winter months. South of Kinder Downfall is **Edale Cross** sitting on a medieval packhorse road from Hayfield via Jacob's Ladder to Edale. Below Kinder Reservoir is **Kinder Quarry**

(now a car park) where the mass trespassers gathered in 1932. A plaque commemorates the event. Nearby is Bowden Bridge, an ancient packhorse bridge, built without side-walls as these interfered with the horses' panniers.

There is also a large area of the Peak District that exists to the north of Longdendale. While much of it consists of moorland there are many interesting and picturesque valleys that await exploration. Unfortunately the area is also well served by reservoirs as a quick look at the ordnance map reveals. It is an area certainly well worth discovering by car and there are plenty of opportunities for including a short walk in your itinerary.

If one parks in Holme village, a footpath leads northwards towards Digley Reservoir and crosses the water at its western end. The path climbs up to an old track and then one can walk above the northern shore of the reservoir towards the National Park car park at Digley Quarry. The road may then be taken over the dam and back to Holme. As you walk up the road towards the village look carefully at the capstones on the wall on your left. There are several lots of twin holes in the stones. These originally held tenter hooks and were used for drying cloth.

South-west of Holmfirth, and conspicuous for miles, is a modern windmill used for generating electricity at a local dairy. This is where Longley Farm dairy products such as yoghurt are manufactured.

Walks around Kinder

Certain routes are suggested here in brief outline. It must be stressed again that the moors should not be crossed without adequate clothing, boots, food, drink and with a compass and map. Also consult the local weather forecast and advise someone of your plans before setting out.

Hayfield, Kinder Downfall, Edale Cross 10 miles (16km)

From Hayfield take the road to Kinder Reservoir and then take the path up the northern side of the reservoir along White Brow. Proceed up William Clough to the cairn at the top and then walk along the edge of Kinder Scout (also the Pennine Way here) to Kinder Downfall. Return via Edale Cross and Tunstead Clough Farm.

Edale, Grindsbrook Clough 9 miles (14.4km)

From the car park just before Edale village, close to the railway station, walk up the road through the village towards Grindsbrook and Kinder Scout. Cross the brook on a log bridge and walk up the valley, eventually leaving the pasture. Gradually Edale Valley disappears from view and the path hugs the brook up onto the Kinder plateau. Follow the Pennine Way to Kinder Downfall. Return via Edale Cross and Jacob's Ladder to Upper Booth and then across fields to Edale. The views from Upper Grindsbrook and on the descent from Jacob's Ladder are particularly memorable.

Alport Bridge, Howden Reservoir, Hagg Farm 8 miles (12.8km)

This walk is not actually on Kinder Scout but in the area on the opposite side of the Snake Pass. From Alport Bridge, (SK143896) just upstream from Hagg Farm, on the A57 west of Ladybower Reservoir, take the track up to Alport Farm. Skirt the farm buildings and cross the brook before climbing up onto Birchinlee Pasture. The path follows Alport Castles Edge giving good views down Alport Dale and over to Kinder Scout. Take the path across Birchinlee Pasture and drop down the ridge above Ditch Clough into the wood. Walk along the road around to Howden Dam and onto Ouzleden Clough. From here a path climbs up out of the wood. It then follows the top of Gores Plantation, heading for Lockerbrook Farm and Hagg Farm. Alport Bridge lies 1.5 miles (2.4km) up the road.

Above: Crowden Clough, Edale

Left: Kinder Downfall, Kinder Scout

Places to Visit

Eyam

Eyam Museum

Hawkhill Road S32 5QP
☎ 01433 631371
www.eyam.org.uk
Open: 10am–4.30pm Tue–Sun and Bank Holidays (last admin. 4pm), late Mar–early Nov. Tells the history of the village and the time of the plague.
Ⓟnearby ♿ ♔<16 ☀

Eyam Hall

Church Street, Eyam S32 5QW
☎ 01433 631976
www.eyamhall.co.uk
Open: Times vary, see website for details.
Seventeenth-century manor house, restaurant, gift shop and craft centre.
Ⓟ ♿ ♔<5-15 ☀

Derbyshire and Lancashire Gliding Club

Camphill, Gt. Hucklow SK17 8RQ
☎ 01298 871270
www.dlgc.org.uk
Trial flights available or take an activity holiday with a difference – 5-day residential courses offered during the summer months.

Castleton

Peveril Castle

Castleton, Hope Vallwy S33 8WQ.
On south side of village
☎ 01433 620613
www.english-heritage.org.uk
Open: April 10am–5pm; May–Aug 10am–6pm; Sept–Oct 10am–5pm; Winter 10am–4pm; Closed Xmas and 1st Jan
Ⓟnearby ♿shop & interpretation area only ♔<16

Peak Cavern

☎ 01433 620285
www.devilsarse.com
Open: 10am-5pm daily, Apr (or Easter if earlier)–Oct; 10am–5pm weekends only (daily during school holidays), Nov–Mar. Last tour 4pm
Guided tours last about 1 hour and include traditional ropemaking demonstration. Suitable for all ages.

Blue John Cavern

S33 8WP
☎ 01433 620638
www.bluejohn-cavern.co.uk
Open: 9.30am-5.30pm (dusk in winter) daily, all year except Christmas Day. Winter 10am–dusk
Guided tours last 45 mins to 1 hour. Gifts and light refreshments available. No wheelchair access
Ⓟ ♔<5free ☀

Treak Cliff Cavern

S33 8WP
☎ 01433 620571
www.bluejohnstone.com
Open: 10am daily, all year. Last tour Mar–Oct at 4.20pm. Last tour November to February at 3.20pm. Closed Christmas and New Year. Regular special events including 'Polish your own Blue John Stone'. No wheelchair access.
Ⓟ ♔<16 ☀

Speedwell Cavern

Winnats Pass S33 8WA
☎ 01433 620512
www.speedwellcavern.co.uk
Open: Daily except Christmas Day (weather permitting) from 10am–5pm. Last boat leaves 4pm (later at peak times).

Descend 105 steps to the boat landing stage and then travel through the cavern on an underground canal.

Rushup Edge

Chestnut Centre

Castleton Road, Chapel-en-le-Frith SK23 OQS
☎ 01298 814099
www.ottersandowls.co.uk
Open: 10.30-5.30pm daily. Last entrance 4pm Spring/Summer; 3pm Autumn/Winter
Otters and owls living in 50 acres (20.25 hectares) parkland. Tea room and gift shop.

Bradwell

Bagshawe Cavern

Jeffrey Lane
☎ 01433 620540
Now closed to the public and open to cavers only

Hope Valley

Losehill Hall

Hope Valley S33 8WB
☎ 01433 620373
Holiday courses in painting, birdwatching, natural history, walking etc.

Above: Losehill Hall, Castleton

133

The valley of the River Derwent is one of the most pronounced features of the Peak District landscape. The river draws its water initially from the sodden peat hags of Featherbed Moss, where a fan of little streams collect to flow south-east before turning to run in the southerly direction which characterises much of its length through the Peak. The valley soon becomes deeply entrenched, with green fields rising steeply towards the moors. A feature down the length of the valley as far as Chatsworth is the escarpment of gritstone rocks that outcrop on its eastern side. Their total length is around 20 miles (32km) and most can be followed on foot. From the valley these edges dominate the skyline. Now they offer sport to climbers, vantage points to visitors, and an interesting linear path for ramblers.

The Derwent is the major river of the region. In ancient times it must have been a formidable obstacle when in flood. There is a pattern of packhorse routes and saltways crossing the Peak, heading for Sheffield, Chesterfield and places to the east, all having to descend to and cross the Derwent. Bridges were therefore built at an early date; the existing bridge at Baslow was built before 1500, while the predecessor of the bridge upstream at Calver was also recorded in the fifteenth century. Derwent village bridge, now re-erected at Slippery Stones, was built in the Middle Ages and it is recorded that it was re-paired in 1682. Downstream, a bridge is recorded at Yorkshire Bridge in 1599 when a wooden structure was rebuilt in stone.

The Derwent Reservoirs

The construction of the Derwent reservoirs has had a significant impact on the upper part of the valley, flooding also the Woodlands Valley, which climbs up the moors toward Snake Pass and Glossop. The **Howden and Derwent dams** were built together, work starting on the former in 1901 and the latter a year later. Howden was finished in 1912 but Derwent took until 1916 to complete. A temporary village was built for the navvies building the dams. It was known as **Birchinlee** and was situated by the present road halfway up the west side of Howden Reservoir. The population rose to over 900 people and it had a shop, hospital, village hall, school and chapel.

Derwent and Ashopton villages were inundated by the rising waters of the Ladybower Reservoir. The remains of Ashopton are now covered by layers of

The Dambusters

Derwent Dam found a new use during World War II, when it was used by RAF 617 squadron for practice runs before the dambusters' raid on Germany and again in the film of the raid. From time to time the RAF pays tribute with a flypast by a Lancaster bomber. Unfortunately such events, including the drought conditions, attract enormous crowds and the roads are choked with traffic. There is a small **Dambusters' Museum** in the west tower of Derwent Dam.

silt, but in times of exceptional drought the outline of **Derwent village** may again be seen. Even the stumps of trees cut down in the 1940s reappear, creating the outline of the original fields. In 1995 the village site was exposed for a considerable period. The outline of the garden to the Hall and the next farm up the valley could be seen quite clearly. Much remains of the Hall foundations and two bridges over the Mill Brook remain, one giving access from the Hall to the church. Here amongst the rubble, the datestone of 1867 remains.

Between the wars, Derwent Hall was used as a youth hostel and was opened by the Prince of Wales in 1932. It was built in 1672 by the Balguy family, but was demolished in 1943 along with Derwent church and village. The church spire was left standing for a few years and the east window was moved to Hathersage Church. The packhorse bridge was placed in store in 1938 and rebuilt in 1959 upstream at Slippery Stones.

Ladybower Reservoir was opened in 1945 by King George VI, having taken ten years to complete, and at the time it was the largest man-made lake in the country. Derwent village was situated roughly where the Mill Brook reached the River Derwent, and Ashopton village was immediately adjacent to Ashopton viaduct and on its south side. It is interesting that even the 1976 Dark Peak tourist map still showed Derwent church tower surrounded by water at SK185886, even though it was demolished in 1947. It was blown up by the Royal Engineers after it was found that divers were finding it a source of attraction. What a pity!

Above the confluence of the Rivers Derwent and Ashop (where the A57 crosses the reservoir) is Crookhill Farm, which was recently acquired by the National Trust. Much closer to the reservoir is a house between the A57 and the water line. The owner refused to sell to the Water Board. The water sometimes rises almost to the old gate at the end of the garden.

Ladybower is popular with anglers fishing for brook, brown and rainbow trout. In 1995 fifty salmon were released into the reservoir to mark the reservoir's 50th anniversary. Day tickets are available.

Man's use of the river and its valley does, of course, go back further. Its water was used to power mills, levels from mines were driven to drain them to the river and quarries have hewn stone for roads, walls, dam construction and millstones. Hundreds of unsold millstones litter the quarries of the eastern edge. Many can be seen at

Millstone Edge on the A625 south-east of Hathersage at SK249799. They lie either side of an old track to Bole Hill Quarry which was reworked to supply stone to Ladybower Dam.

Despite the urbanisation of parts of the valley, there is still much to see which will interest the visitor. The reservoirs have a beauty of their own, and the dams (especially the Derwent Dam) are particularly impressive when overflowing. Unfortunately the woods, which surround the upper two reservoirs, add little harmony to the scene, for they are stark and emphasise a heavy shoreline, particularly when the water level drops. Nonetheless the road from Ashopton viaduct is worth taking to the top of Howden Reservoir. It finishes at a cul-de-dac where there is a path that leads the short distance to **Slippery Stones**.

The **Fairholmes Visitor Centre** incorporates an exhibition on the reservoirs including photographs of Derwent village. There is a tea bar here which also sells hot soup and refreshments, plus toilets as well as the cycle hire centre. Some of the cycles are specially made with a wheelchair on the front.

Hiring a bike at Fairholmes at the southern end of Derwent Reservoir and cycling around the reservoirs is a good way of exploring the area. A suggested route is to go up the valley from Fairholmes on the western side of Derwent Reservoir and on around Howden Reservoir. Return down the eastern side of the valley as far as the Sheffield-Glossop road at the Ashopton viaduct. Cross this and return up the road to Fairholmes. This last section is used by motor vehicles and so care should be exercised, although there is only limited traffic north of Fairholmes and very little on the eastern side of the valley.

Before moving on to the southern part of the valley, it is worth visiting the area to the north-east of the great reservoirs. The valleys here drain into the River Don and thence the Humber quite independently of the Derwent/Trent river system, but they have a character similar to the Upper Derwent Valley, many of them also with reservoirs, albeit on a smaller scale.

The area includes the **Loxley and Ewden valleys** where the moors are lower. Above the Loxley Valley and Strines Reservoir is Boot's Folly, a stone tower built to find work for unemployed men. Much of the moorland has been cultivated, used for plantations or inundated beneath reservoirs. It was here that the Dale Dike Reservoir, upstream of **Low Bradfield**, collapsed when it first filled in 1865. A total of 238 people were drowned and over 600 buildings were destroyed or damaged as the flood swept towards Sheffield.

Park and Ride

On Saturdays, Sundays and Bank Holiday Mondays between Easter and the end of October and on Sundays throughout the winter, visitors must park at Fairholmes, near Derwent Dam (except cars displaying a disabled person's blue badge). To get further up the valley, you must walk, hire a bike or catch the regular minibus service to the King's Tree.

The Derwent Valley & Gritstone Edges

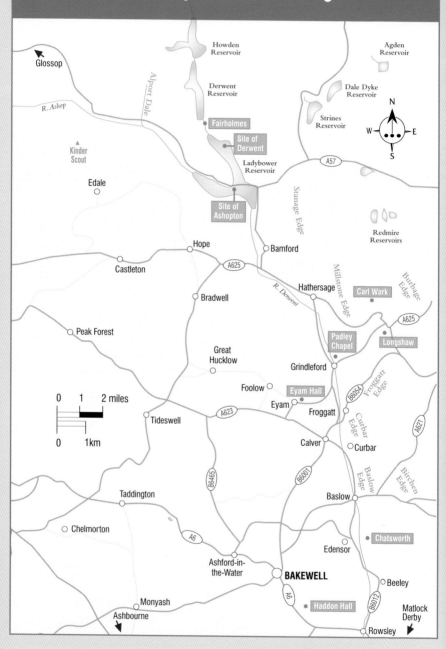

Glossop

Howden Reservoir

Agden Reservoir

R. Ashop

Alport Dale

Derwent Reservoir

Dale Dyke Reservoir

Kinder Scout

Fairholmes

Site of Derwent

Strines Reservoir

N
W · · · E
S

A57

Edale

Ladybower Reservoir

Stanage Edge

Redmire Reservoirs

Site of Ashopton

Hope

Bamford

Castleton

A625

Millstone Edge

Burbage Edge

Bradwell

R. Derwent

Hathersage

Carl Wark

Peak Forest

A625

Great Hucklow

Padley Chapel

Longshaw

Grindleford

Froggatt Edge

Foolow

Eyam Hall

B6054

0 1 2 miles

Tideswell

A623

Eyam

Froggatt

Curbar Edge

A621

0 1km

Calver

Curbar

Taddington

B6465

B6001

Baslow Edge

Birchen Edge

Chelmorton

A6

Baslow

Chatsworth

Edensor

Ashford-in-the-Water

BAKEWELL

Beeley

Monyash

A6

Haddon Hall

B6012

Matlock Derby

Ashbourne

Rowsley

6. The Derwent Valley and the Gritstone Edges

Derwent Reservoir

Hathersage from above Froggatt

Derwent Valley World Heritage Site

Although outside the Peak District National Park boundary, most of this area is seen as very much part of the Peak District and many places have already been described in earlier chapters. The Derwent Valley from Matlock Bath downstream to Derby is considered to be the birthplace of the factory system, where water power was first harnessed to power textile manufacture, leading in part to the Industrial Revolution. The importance of this area was internationally recognised in December 2001 when UNESCO designated it a World Heritage Site. The citation read:

The cultural landscape of the Derwent Valley is of outstanding significance because it was here that the modern factory system was established to accommodate the new technology for spinning cotton developed by Richard Arkwright. The insertion of industrial establishments into a rural landscape necessitated the construction of housing for the workers at the mills, and the resulting settlements created an exceptional industrial landscape that has retained its qualities over two centuries.

It was not just the factories themselves that changed the area but also the services that were needed to support them such as roads, railways and canals. Quarries were opened to produce building stone and road stone. Today it is possible to see many of these places although apart from the A6 road through the valley, all are much quieter and largely used for recreational purposes.

Take a journey from Derby up to Matlock Bath stopping along the way to visit places such as **Derby Silk Mill, Milford Mill** – originally owned by the Strutt family - and **Belper –** with its nailmaker's cottages, Long Row built by Jedediah Strutt for his workers and East Mill. Then on to **Ambergate** where the **Cromford Canal** is seen for the first time.

From there to Matlock Bath look out for Leawood Pumping Station, Cromford Wharf and the beginning of the Cromford and High Peak Railway, workers' cottages of the period in Cromford, Arkwright's Mill and Masson Mill. (See earlier chapters for details) All these and more are part of the story of the Derwent Valley.

Derwent Valley Heritage Way

The River Derwent starts its journey, to its confluence with the river Trent near Shardlow, on the moors above Slippery Stones. A new 55-mile (88.5km) walking route, the **Derwent Valley Heritage Way**, has been devised to follow this journey allowing walkers to appreciate the lovely landscape and see the industrial heritage on the way. It can be walked as a long-distance path or in sections when time permits, using public transport to return to the day's starting point. On the first day that it was officially opened two men covered the distance in one day but it will be better appreciated at a much slower pace!

The walk starts at the southern end of Ladybower Reservoir keeping as near to the river as possible. It is a fairly level walk passing through fields and woodland, on some pavements and roads, and may be flooded in places if the river is very high. It goes on via Hathersage, Grindleford, Baslow, Rowsley, Matlock, Cromford, Belper, and Derby before finishing where the Derwent finishes, at its meeting with the Trent near Shardlow. Some of the trail is accessible by wheelchairs including the first stretch, where the new **Thornhill Trail** has been created along the track of the old railway used to take building stone to the dams.

The trail is waymarked throughout by yellow arrows on a purple background and is well served by public transport. It offers an excellent way of experiencing the Derwent Valley Mills World Heritage Site, mostly away from the modern road system, so that walkers can more easily imagine the scene when all the mills were working, the canals were transporting goods and raw materials and no doubt the valley was alive with very different sounds to those of today.

Brontë associations

The association with Charlotte Brontë deserves better recognition in the village. She stayed at the vicarage with Ellen Nussey, the sister of the rector, in 1845. Henry Nussey wanted to marry Charlotte but she declined him, in the same way as Jane Eyre declined St John Rivers. Eyre is a local name and Moor House has been identified as being based upon Moorseats, partly thirteenth century but largely rebuilt in 1682. Likewise, North Lees Hall features as Thornfield Hall. It was rebuilt in 1594-6.

Above Low Bradfield, with its village cricket pitch, is **High Bradfield**. Here there is a motte and bailey castle and an interesting church, which retains its former watch house, built to deter body snatchers and now converted to a small dwelling. A trip around the area, including the ancient Strines Inn, Bolsterstone, Ewden and the Bradfield village is recommended if you can follow the little lanes on a motoring map.

A little to the north of this area is the tiny village of Langsett, with the **Langsett Barn National Park Visitor Centre** on the A616 between Stocksbridge and Holmfirth. Housed in a restored seventeenth-century aisled barn, there are displays about the 120 acre (48 hectare) Langsett Reservoir, completed in 1904. The valve tower on the dam has a castellated top and is a replica of a tower at Lancaster Castle!

Above: Old trough left incomplete, with Carl Wark in the background
Below: View of Hathersage

Hathersage and the Hope Valley

The Lower Derwent and the Gritstone Edges

Some 4 miles (6.4km) south-east of Ladybower Reservoir is **Hathersage**. It has associations with Charlotte Brontë who wove her novel Jane Eyre around the area, calling the town Morton.

In the churchyard is the gravestone of Little John, the friend and companion of Robin Hood. Apparently he was a native of Hathersage, was known as John Little, and made his living as a nailer until he found everlasting fame. The town has a passenger railway station on the line between Sheffield and Manchester, which also has stations at Grindleford, Bamford, Hope and Edale. There is a coaching inn in the town centre – the George – which has an interesting old cheese press by the side of the road.

The church was built in 1381 and Pevsner asserts that the chancel and south arcade are possibly of this date. He describes the fifteenth-century brasses

143

as 'excellent'. As related above, the east window comes from the demolished church at Derwent village. Hathersage has some rather fine stone-built properties, a good outdoor centre, an outdoor swimming pool – a rarity these days, and several shops and banks.

Tucked away on the B6001 out of Hathersage towards Grindleford is **The Round Building,** a factory with a difference. David Mellor cutlery is made in a purpose-built, circular building, which nestles into the surrounding landscape. Visitors are welcome to see the cutlery being made and there is a cook shop where a professional range of kitchenware is sold alongside other examples of fine British crafts for the kitchen.

Leaving Hathersage towards Sheffield, the road climbs up to Millstone Edge. Just before the sharp bend with its viewpoint – approached from the opposite direction the valley suddenly opens up before you and you will appreciate why it is known as **Surprise View** – there is a National Trust sign on the right marked Bole Hill.

A path runs down an old railway track into the wood where there are hundreds of abandoned millstones. Although this is the largest concentration, they can be found scattered along all the gritstone edges above the eastern side of the Derwent Valley.

Millstones were sent from here to places as far away as Russia, but the trade suddenly collapsed in the nineteenth century with the introduction of new methods of grinding corn, and the already finished stones were abandoned. Some, shaped like a mushroom cap, are much older and it is not clear why these were discarded. Whilst you are inspecting the Bole Hill millstones, look out for the wood ants nests. These small ant hills are everywhere! The ants are so numerous that they completely preclude any ideas of sitting in the grass, especially for a picnic.

Proceeding down into the wood beyond the millstones, one reaches the remains of a large quarry, now being regenerated by silver birch trees. This is where the stone for the Howden and Derwent dams was quarried. There used to be a steep inclined railway down into the valley to enable the railway trucks to reach the temporary line that took the stone up the valley to the dams.

With the huge quarry on Eldon Hill near Mam Tor having closed in March 1997, it is reassuring to know that such scars on the landscape can be effectively screened as has happened here. Given time and perhaps some helpful reclamation work to assist the process, we can leave the rest to nature.

South of the town the Burbage Brook flows through **Padley Gorge** to join the Derwent at Grindleford. The descent of the brook through the wood is steep and the brook rushes amid boulders and trees in a steep-sided valley. This is a beauty spot missed by many visitors who overlook it. It is best visited by walking upstream to get the best views of the rushing white water. The 3.5 mile (5.6km) walk starts by a bus stop on the B6521, immediately above Grindleford Station, where a stile gives access to the wood. The path is easy to follow and, upon passing through a gate, drops down a series of steps to a footbridge. Once over the brook, the path climbs steeply to an elevated level above the stream. Eventually the path leaves the wood and crosses through flat fields to reach the A625.

Ahead lies Stanage Edge and by the main road, **Toad's Mouth Rock**, a curious natural rock formation overlooked by **Carl Wark**, a hill fort of the Iron Age. It has a huge platform built of gritstone blocks up to 5ft (1.5m) across and ramparts 10ft (3m) high. To the south is the **Longshaw Estate**, purchased from the Duke of Rutland by subscription and given to the National Trust when he sold his 11,500 acre (4,600 hectare) estate here in 1927. A path returns to Grindleford through the estate, past the house and its lake. This is the site for the Longshaw Sheepdog Trials held every September. There is a **National Trust Information Centre**, shop and cafeteria at Longshaw.

Before leaving the Longshaw area the **chapel at Padley** should not be missed. This is reached by taking the unmade track beyond Grindleford Railway Station. It is the final remnant of Padley Hall whose excavated foundations can be seen at the rear. The hall

Padley Chapel

Two priests were arrested here on 12 July 1588 and subsequently executed at Derby. The chapel fell into disuse, but was restored in 1933 after the discovery of the altar. A remembrance service for the 'Padley Martyrs' is held here annually on the Thursday nearest to 12 July.

was built in the fourteenth and fifteenth centuries by the Catholic FitzHerbert family. It may also be visited by prior appointment.

Although this old house has been demolished, a link with this era and this family does survive. A branch of the FitzHerberts built Norbury Manor (near Ashbourne) in about 1250, enlarging it in 1305. This old house may be seen adjacent to the church, at the rear of the much later house to which it is attached.

The gritstone edges are a prominent geological feature east of the River Derwent. Outstanding examples are Birchen Edge, Gardom's Edge, Baslow Edge, Curbar Edge, Froggatt Edge, Millstone Edge, Burbage Edge and Stanage Edge. There are paths along the tops of most of these edges and all give spectacular views. Many are popular with rock climbers. On Birchen Edge is **Nelson's Monument**, erected in 1810 by a local man, while **Baslow Edge** has a monument to Wellington erected in 1866. Near to Nelson's Monument are three huge rocks looking like ships with the names Victory, Defiant, and Royal Soverin (sic) on their bows, unusual in an area so far from the sea.

In the valley bottom below the gritstone edges lie the villages of Calver and Baslow. That part of **Calver**, by the traffic lights and known as Calver Sough, takes its name from an old lead mine, last worked in the mid-nineteenth century when a steam pumping engine was erected close to the crossroads. Just to the north of Calver is Stoke Hall. There is an attractive walk between the bridges at Froggatt and Calver. A path follows each side of the river and makes a good circular walk. It is easier to park near Calver Bridge than at Froggatt. The river is deep, wide and slow moving and the broad expanse of water looks very attractive on a sunny day. The former cotton mill at Calver was built by Richard Arkwright in 1803-4 and was used to film the television series *Colditz*. Near the fine eighteenth-century stone bridge is a craft centre with a bookshop and cafeteria.

Above Calver's bridge on the eastern side of the valley is the village of Curbar. Marked on the Ordnance Survey map are the graves of the Cundy family, victims of the plague. They date from 1632 and five interments lie beneath rough-hewn slabs of limestone. Nearby and a little further down the hillside is an unusual building, square with a conical stone slab roof. It was used as a lock-up and then a dwelling until 1935.

Baslow

A walk along the gritstone edges

These edges offer the opportunity for a marvellous linear walk from the signposted path by a stile on the Baslow side of the Robin Hood Inn on the A619 (SK277722). The path cuts around Gardom's Edge and then crosses the A621 heading for Wellington's Monument. From here it follows Baslow, Curbar and Froggatt Edges, passing a small stone circle by Froggatt Edge. The views along the edges down into the Derwent Valley and across to Eyam Moor and Longstone Moor are marvellous.

It is difficult to appreciate that the outskirts of Sheffield are only 4 miles (7km) away. A footpath to Nether Padley leads to Padley Gorge and the climb back towards Stanage Edge, which winds around to Moscar above Bamford Moor and Ladybower Reservoir. However, this walk ends 15 miles (24km) from the start, so another car or a helpful second driver is needed. Alternatively a series of separate walks along the individual edges may be planned.

Curbar Gap

Although on private ground, a footpath in a nearby field comes close to it.

Baslow is divided into Over End, Nether End and Bridge End. At the latter there is an interesting medieval bridge with a very small guard house, just large enough for one person to collect tolls. The nearby church has an unusual clock with 'VICTORIA 1897' instead of numerals, while inside is a dog whip used to chase stray dogs out during church services.

Most visitors to Baslow are attracted to Nether End with its little shops set around a green. Beyond the impressive Cavendish Hotel is a car park. If you prefer a 1.5 mile (2.4km) walk to Chatsworth, park here. Cross the little brook a few yards eastwards from the car park and take the signposted path down the brookside past a rare sight in this area – a thatched cottage. The path crosses the river meadows and reaches Chatsworth by Queen Mary's Bower and the elegant bridge over the river.

The luxuriously appointed Cavendish Hotel is owned by the Chatsworth Estate and many of the furnishings came from the House. It was owned by the Duke of Rutland until the two estates exchanged lands in the 1830s. It has 23 bedrooms overlooking the Chatsworth Estate.

Chatsworth

Chatsworth, the home of the Cavendish family, is one of the Wonders of the Peak and one of the finest houses in Britain. The son of William Cavendish and Bess of Hardwick was created the first Earl of Devonshire and his descendant, the fourth Earl, was created the first Duke of Devonshire for sup-

porting the cause of William of Orange. Bess of Hardwick brought considerable wealth to the Cavendish family and with the dissolution of the monasteries, this wealth was used to purchase land on a large scale throughout the Peak District and elsewhere.

The wealth from landed property was augmented, chiefly during the eighteenth century, by considerable royalties from lead mines in the Peak District and also from copper ores from the Duke's mine at Ecton in the Manifold Valley. Between 1760 and 1792, the Ecton mine alone produced an estimated profit of £294,000, and this enormous income helped create an extremely wealthy dynasty. As a consequence, Chatsworth is a treasure house, richly endowed with old masters, priceless furniture, tapestries, carvings and porcelain.

Today it is open to visitors and the route taken through the house includes the majority of the main state rooms on the south front. Much of the present house was built by the first and sixth dukes, ie in the seventeenth century and in the early part of the nineteenth century. It therefore makes an interesting comparison with the older Haddon Hall. Perhaps one of the most inter-

Special lawns

The two large lawns (known as the Salisbury Lawns) have received no chemicals in over 200 years and are full of herbs. Such is their importance, the Botanical Department at Sheffield University brings students to study these lawns.

esting aspects of Chatsworth is that a considerable number of its treasures are on display. Everywhere one goes in the house there are priceless and beautiful works of art. You should allow plenty of time for a walk around Chatsworth. There is so much that otherwise will be missed such as the wood and alabaster carvings in the chapel and the violin in the music room. At the end of the tour there is a shop in the former orangery, which leads out into the garden.

Upon leaving the house a huge conservatory runs up the side of the garden wall, with various fruit trees growing inside. Nearby, although not usually open, is a modern hothouse. It is full of tropical plants including a huge Amazonian lily. Chatsworth is proud that this plant first flowered here in 1851, ahead of the one at Kew! The first Duke's greenhouse is now full of camellias, which the Duke exhibits at the Royal Horticultural Society's show in March each year.

If you wander off on the paths beyond the Cascade, look out for the Willow Tree fountain and beyond it the **Rock Garden**. The latter was built by Joseph Paxton and it has recently been restored to its full glory to celebrate the 200th anniversary of his birth in 1803. In 2003 a new sensory garden was opened and visitors will find a collection of Elizabeth Frink sculptures in the garden, including the latest – the 'Walking Madonna'.

The 106 acre (42.4 hectare) garden is also worthy of a visit. It should be given at least half a day in order to explore the various points of interest. It includes the **Emperor Fountain,** set in its canal pond and noted for being the highest gravity fed fountain in the world, rising to a height of 260ft (80m). Elsewhere in the gardens is the maze, set on the site of what used to be the conservatory built by Paxton and a forerunner of his Crystal Palace, which was built in London for the Great Exhibition of 1851.

Behind the house are the **Cascade** and the aqueduct, together with Stand Wood with its various footpaths along the valley side. In springtime the woods are full of bluebells and spring flowers. The Cascade has 24 steps and has recently been restored, with some 54 tons of new stone replacing old and eroded stone. As each step is of varying dimensions, the water makes a different sound as it falls over the steps. A new addition to the list of attractions is a series of Behind the Scenes days. These enable you to see what goes on in various aspects of estate life such as the garden, estate and the collection. It is necessary to book these events in advance.

Above the Stand Wood can be seen the **Prospect Tower**, a relic of the Elizabethan manor house that existed here before the present house was built. A more recent innovation has been the development of a forestry and farming display plus an adventure playground, which is always a special treat for children. By the forestry exhibition is a ten-ton pile of timber, representing just 24 hours' growth on the estate's 2,500 acres (1,000 hectare) of woodland. There are no lions and safari parks here, but there are several festivals at different times of the year, which can add immensely to a visit to this delightful place.

Adjacent to the car park is the former stable block that has now been converted into a restaurant, cafe and a

Chatsworth House

Opposite: Edensor, where all the houses are of different styles
Opposite below: Chatsworth, The Painted Hall (Trustees of The Chatsworth Settlement)

151

large shop. With Chatsworth's annual overheads exceeding £1,000,000, all these various enterprises help to contribute to the upkeep of this national treasure.

In May, Chatsworth hosts one of the largest Angling Fairs in Britain, at which there are numerous demonstrations and trade stands. Each September, the Chatsworth Country Fair is held. There is a full programme of events together with over 300 trade stands. This huge fair opens at 8.30am on each of the two days of the event.

If you like to ramble, do not overlook Chatsworth Park. There are several private paths through the park to which the public are permitted access and these are shown on notice boards. If you are south of the house itself, look out for the deer on the east bank of the river. At the southern end of the park, close to One Arch Bridge (with traffic lights), is Calton Lees picnic area and car park set amid the trees above the road. It is a useful place to park if exploring the estate paths. There is a tea bar and the estate sells a leaflet about its Stand Wood walks, which take you above and behind Chatsworth House.

In Stand Wood you can walk in comparative quietness around the lakes that supply water to the garden. Quite a long walk can be planned if you so wish. The path climbs up through the wood to the Hunting Lodge.

Close to Chatsworth is **Edensor** village, built in 1838-42 by Joseph Paxton to house the inhabitants of the original village. All the houses are of different styles and the church, built in 1867, stands in a dominating situation above the houses. It is rather dark inside and you may need to turn on the lights to view it properly. There is an interesting display on the redevelopment of the village, together with a leaflet for sale explaining much more. Although it is often thought that the whole of the village – bar one house – was demolished, this is not the case. All the main street was demolished except one house, which now stands in isolation. Several others were altered including the former eighteenth-century inn near to the Post Office where there is now a tea room. The leaflet and the display enables you to appreciate the full extent of the redevelopment undertaken by the sixth Duke.

Exploring the church, one can still see the everlasting flowers of the wreath sent by Queen Victoria when Lord Frederick Cavendish was buried following his assassination in Phoenix Park, Dublin in 1882. There is also a huge monument in the same chapel to two sons of Bess of Hardwick dating from the seventeenth century.

Halfway up the churchyard is the tomb of Joseph Paxton who spent much of his life at Chatsworth marrying a local girl, Sarah, who is buried with him. He was a close friend as well as an employee of the sixth Duke. At the top of the churchyard are some of the Devonshire family tombs (many earlier ones are in Derby Cathedral) including Kathleen Kennedy, the sister of the late US President. She was married to the Marquis of Hartington, the eldest son of the tenth Duke of Devonshire, and was killed in a plane crash. Unfortunately her husband pre-deceased her, having been killed in World War II.

President Kennedy came to Chatsworth in 1963 to visit his sister's grave. A marble slab marks the spot where he tendered his last respects before his own untimely death. Just north of Edensor (pronounced Ensor) is **Pilsley**, where some of the relocated villagers were rehoused. However the village is not as attractive as Edensor. The Chatsworth estate has a **farmshop** here and there are also craft shops and a tearoom.

Places to Visit

Ⓟ Parking Available
♿ Disabled Facilities
👪 Family Attraction
<№ Concession for under certain ages
☂ Suitable in Wet Weather

Derwent Valley Reservoirs

Dambusters' Museum

West tower of Derwent Dam
Open: 10am–4pm every Sun and Bank Holiday Monday.
Memorabilia from the training sessions held here and the making of the film. Admission free.

Upper Derwent Visitor Centre

Upper Derwent Lane, Bamford S33 OAQ. Near Derwent Dam
☎ 01433 650953
Open: daily Easter–end-Oct. Weekends only in the winter.
Information, cycle hire, light refreshments.

Hathersage

David Mellor Design

The Round Building, Hathersage, Sheffield S32 1BA. B6001 out of Hathersage
☎01433 650220
www.davidmellordesign.co.uk
Open: Shop – 10am–5pm Mon–Sat, 11am–5pm on Sun. Tours of the factory are usually possible.

Grindleford

Longshaw Estate Visitor Centre (National Trust)

S11 7TZ
☎ 01433 637904
www.nationaltrust.org.uk
Open: daily,10.30am–5pm, mid March–end Oct; weekends only Nov–Mar 10.30am–4pm. National Trust shop, tea room, visitor centre.
Ⓟcharge ♿not walks 👪free

Chatsworth

Chatsworth House

Bakewell DE45 1PJ
☎ 01246 565300
www.chatsworth.org
Open: 11am-5.30pm daily Mid-Mar–late-Dec.
Magnificent home of the Duke of Devonshire, more than 30 rooms containing priceless paintings, furniture, silver, tapestries and porcelain. Restaurant, shops, farmyard and adventure playground. House specially decorated in the weeks before Christmas.
Gardens open as house but close at 6pm and open at 10.30am in Jun, Jul and Aug.
Ⓟcharge ♿ 👪 ☂

7. Around the Peak District

Although the Peak District is a relatively small area, given good weather conditions it would take more than one holiday in the National Park to visit all its various attractions. But if one is unfortunate enough to visit the Peak during a spell of wet weather and have already visited the major outdoor attractions detailed in the various chapters of this book, then you might wish to look slightly further afield.

On all sides of the Peak District there are adventure parks, stately homes (some, such as Hardwick Hall and Kedleston Hall, are of national importance), museums and steam railways, which justify a visit. As this book takes

a liberal view as to the definition of the Peak District, it is not confined to the strict boundaries of the National Park. Some of these places, such as Alton Towers and the country houses on the Cheshire fringe, have been included in earlier chapters. Here are some other suggestions for places to visit.

If the weather is good you may find yourself with a different problem! The large number of visitors to the Peak results in too many people arriving at the more popular centres, especially on Bank Holidays. On Easter Monday 1997, it was reported that gridlock had occured at Wetton Mill and Dovedale car parks through excessive numbers of

vehicles. They were so tightly packed that a police motor cyclist could not penetrate.

On that day, it was quite easy to move around the Goyt Valley, despite a lot of people enjoying themselves there. Further to the west, between Forest Chapel and Jenkin Chapel, there were hardly any more vehicles than usual. Excessive vehicle numbers were also reported in Matlock, Matlock Bath and Bakewell.

There are plenty of areas where congestion does not occur and the purpose of this book is to highlight where lovely scenery may be enjoyed away from the most popular areas. One such area is **The National Forest**, currently being developed in south Derbyshire and north Leicestershire. This is till a relatively quiet area but there are many places of interest to visit for young and old alike.

Cheshire

Quarry Bank Mill and Styal Country Estate (National Trust)

Wilmslow
☎ 01625 445896
Open: 11am–5pm daily Mar–end Oct;. 11am–4pm Wed– Sun, Nov–mid-Dec and Jan; daily 28th Dec-3 Jan.
Working Georgian water-powered cotton mill, apprentice house, village of Styal where workers were housed. Farmland and woodland walks on the estate. Children's playground, restaurant.

Chesterfield

Bolsover Castle

Castle St., Bolsover S44 6PR
Off M1 at J29 or 30.
☎ 01246 822844
www.English-heritage.org.uk
Open: 10am–5pm daily, April–end Oct (6pm in July-Aug);10am-4pm Thu–Mon, Nov–Mar.
Discovery Centre, video and audio tour, wall paintings, 'Garden of Love', shop, tea room.

Chesterfield Museum

St Mary's Gate
☎ 01246 345727
Open: 10am-4pm Mon, Tue, Thu, Fri and Sat, all year.
Story of Chesterfield from Roman times to present day. Medieval builders' wheel. George Stephenson memorabilia.
Admission free

Hardwick Hall (National Trust)

S44 5QJ
Off M1 at J29
☎ 01246 850431
Open: 12pm–6pm, Wed, Thu, Sat and Sun, late-Apr–late-Sep and Bank Holidays (Oct 10am–5pm). Parkland open all year
Magnificent Elizabethan house built by Bess of Hardwick. Lovely gardens, shop, tea room.

Hardwick Old Hall (English Heritage)

Doe Lea, Chesterfield S44 5QJ
Off M1 at J29
☎ 01246 850431
Open: mid Mar–end Oct, Wed–Sun, 10am–5pm (Oct 10am–5pm)
Birthplace of Bess of Hardwick. Stately ruin next to Hardwick Hall (National Trust).

Derby

Calke Abbey (National Trust)

Ticknall, 8 miles (12.8km) south of Derby
☎ 01332 863822
Open: 12.30pm–5pm Sat–Wed, Mar–end Oct. Garden and stables 11am–5pm, (closed Thur–Fri, but open daily July–Aug). Timed tickets for the house at busy times. Parkland open all year. The 'House that time forgot'. Little restored, contains amazing collections built up by Harpur Crewe family. Walled garden, extensive parkland, restaurant, shop.

Kedleston Hall (National Trust)

Kedleston4 miles (6.4km) north-west of Derby
☎ 01332 842191
Open : 12noon-5pm Sat–Wed, Mar–Oct. Garden and park 10am–6pm daily for the same period.
Classical Palladian mansion of the 18th century with Robert Adam interiors. Park also designed by Adam. Restaurant and shop.

Sudbury Hall (National Trust)

Sudbury, Ashbourne, Derbyshire DE6 5HT 10 miles (16.25km) east of Derby on A50.
☎ 01283 585305
Open: 1–5pm Wed–Sun, Mar–Oct. Grounds open at 11am.
Charles II house with fine late seventeenth-century decoration. Museum of Childhood. Shop and tea room.

Ⓟ ♿ ⋔Museum, Hall/Gardens involve steps ☃

Derby Museums

www.derby.gov.uk/services/museums
All open: 11am–5pm Mon; 10am–5pm Tue–Sat; 1-4pm Sun and Bank Holidays.

Industrial Museum

Silk Mill Road, Derby DE1 3AF
☎ 01332 255308
Derbyshire industries, including Rolls-Royce aero engines.

Museum and Art Gallery

The Strand, Derby DE1 1BS
☎ 01332 641901
Local history, archaeology, natural history, Derby ceramics, Derbyshire clocks and paintings by Joseph Wright.

Pickford's House

41 Friar Gate, Derby DE1 1DA
☎ 01332 255363
Restored Georgian town house with period interiors and furniture. Changing exhibitions.

National Forest

Conkers

Rawdon Road, Moira, Swadlincote, Derbys DE12 6GA
☎ 01283 216633
www.visitconkers.com
Open: 10am–6pm (5pm in winter), daily all year (not Christmas Day).
Hands on experience at the heart of the National Forest visitor centre. Indoor and outdoor interactive experiences with a woodland theme. Assault course, adventure playground, tree canopy walk, restaurants and shops.
There are many other places to visit in the National Forest plus cycle trails, walks and canals. Full details can be obtained from the National Forest Company ☎ 01283 551211 www.nationalforest.org

Ripley

Midland Railway Centre

Butterley Station, Butterley, Ripley, Derby DE5 3QZ, on B6179 one mile (1.6km) north of Ripley, off M1 J28.
☎ 01773 747674
www.midlandrailwaycentre.co.uk
Open: Most weekends and other days including special events. Times vary (telephone). Trains usually run from 11.15am.
Passenger trains operate on 3.5mile (5.6km) preserved railway. Museum and animal farm, model railway, narrow gauge and miniature railway.

Sheffield

Abbeydale Industrial Hamlet

Abbeydale Rd, Sheffield, 4 miles (6.4km) south of city centre on A621
☎ 0114 272 2106
Open: 10am–4pm Mon–Thu; 11am–4.45pm Sun, early-Apr–early-Oct.
Historic steel working site showing how steel was produced, how the workers lived and how the machinery was powered. Interactive exhibits.

Bishop's House

Meersbrook Park, Norton, Sheffield.
☎ 0114 278 2600
www.shef.ac.uk/city/museums/bishop
Open: 10am–4.30pm Sat, 11am–4.30pm Sun.
Earliest and best preserved example of a timber-framed building in the area.

Sheffield Industrial Museum

Kelham Island, Alma Street, Sheffield.
☎ 0114 272 2106
Open 10am–4pm Mon–Thu; 11am–4.45pm Sun, all year.
The story of Sheffield's industrial evolution with displays, films and workshops. Rolling mill engine run on steam daily. Working craftsmen.

Stoke-on-Trent

Gladstone Pottery Museum

Uttoxeter Road, Longton ST3 1PQ
☎ 01782 237777
www.stoke.gov.uk/Gladstone
Open: 10am–5pm daily, all year.
Unique Victorian pottery factory. Hands-on displays, make your own flower in china clay. Shop and tea room.

The Potteries Museum and Art Gallery

Bethesda Street, Hanley ST1 3DW
☎ 01782 232323
www.stoke.gov.uk/museums
Open: Times vary (telephone)
One of the world's finest collection of ceramics plus the story of the Potteries and a Mark XVI Spitfire. Shop and tea room.

Wedgwood Visitor Centre

Barlaston, south of the city ST12 9ES.
☎ 01782 204218/0870 606 1759
www.thewedgwoodstory.com
Open: 9am–5pm Mon–Fri, 10am–5pm Sat–Sun.
Facilities include a film show, shop, museum, personal audio factory tour, shops and 2 restaurants.

For a more comprehensive list of potteries open to the public contact Stoke-on-Trent TIC ☎ 01782 236000.

Wedgwood Museum

Barlaston, Stoke on Trent, ST12 9ES.
☎ 01782 371900
Open daily, 9am–5pm, Mon–Fri; 10am–5pm, Sat–Sun. Closed over Xmas.

8. Scenic Routes for Motorists

With carefully selected routes it is possible to gain a good impression of the general beauty of the Peak District from your car. Five scenic routes have been chosen with this in mind. They cover main trunk roads and also quiet back lanes generally used only by local farmers. It must be emphasised that many visiting motorists using these roads do so with no apparent regard for safety. Please drive at a speed commensurate with the width of the road and visibility. Hug the inside of bends and approach each one expecting to meet an oncoming vehicle. Some farmers drive cattle along the road on foot, especially before and after milking time, so bear this in mind too. Each route is picked for its picturesque views and many of the byroads will be comparatively quiet mid-week. It is assumed that the reader will also use a map, although directions are fairly comprehensive.

Bakewell, Ashbourne and the Dove Valley

This route takes you past Chatsworth and through the southern limestone plateau to Ashbourne, returning via the Dove Valley. It takes approximately two hours and is about 50 miles (80km) in length.

Take the A619 to Sheffield and then

Opposite page: Winnats Pass
Left: Bridge at Alton

the B6048, passing Pilsley and the Chatsworth Farm shop to the B6012. Turn right to Chatsworth Park and Edensor, the model village built by the Duke of Devonshire. If you wish to visit the village, turn right over the cattle grid, which is almost level with the church. The road continues, with views of Chatsworth House to your left, reaching the A6 at Rowsley. Turn right here, passing the Peacock Hotel on your right, and Caudwell's Flour Mill on your left. Proceed for 1.5 miles (2.4km) or so and take the B5056 to your left (signposted to Ashbourne).

The B5056 follows the River Lathkill and after 1 mile (1.6km) the road swings to the left over the river before entering a long and pleasant wooded stretch. After a while you may detour into Birchover or Winster if you wish to visit the Old Market Hall, now owned by the National Trust. Continue along the B5056 past the Miner's Standard pub and onto its junction with the A5012, the Via Gellia road. Go straight across and, after 2 miles (3.2km), go under the High Peak Trail bridge. Look carefully on your left and right now for small pillars of dolomitic limestone as you wend your way downhill. After 3 miles (4.8km) turn right; you will be faced by a ford where the Bradbourne Brook crosses the road. If you prefer not to risk crossing the ford, continue down the B5056 until it reaches the A515 and then turn left for Ashbourne. Otherwise, proceed through the water and then test your brakes. Climb up the hill and into Tissington to explore the village with its lovely hall. Leave the village and, on reaching the A515, turn left for Ashbourne.

Ashbourne currently has inadequate summertime parking facilities and if the central Shaw Croft car park is full, go to Cokayne Avenue car park just beyond the park if you intend to stop here. It is further out of town, but you will save on time spent looking for a place in which to park. Upon leaving, take Union Street at the top of the market place, which proceeds into Dovehouse Green. This soon bears to the right (into North Avenue), but go straight on over the brow into the road to Mapleton, passing Callow Hall which is now a restaurant. Follow the signs into Thorpe and then head for Ilam, descending to the River Dove below the Izaak Walton Hotel, with the entrance to Dovedale on your right.

On reaching Ilam, turn right at the village cross and take the road to Alstonefield. The road climbs out of the village with views on your left to Throwley and the Manifold Valley. After 3 miles (4.8km), turn right and then left at Hopedale. Climb up into Alstonefield, but carry on at the junction by the old school to the next T-junction and then turn left for Hulme End. Continue along this road until you reach the Manifold Valley Hotel at Hulme End. Turn right for Hartington on the B5054 and, on reaching there, bear left past the duck pond on the gated road for Pilsbury. This quiet road runs up the Dove Valley and climbs sharply up the valley side at Pilsbury, just after it passes the farm. Go over the crossroads, under the Tissington Trail (ex-railway) bridge to reach the A515. Turn left and then right for Monyash, and then return to Bakewell on the B5055.

Deep Valleys and High Moorland of the mid-Peak

Views into Monsal Dale and the Derwent Valley are followed by an exploration of part of the eastern moorlands before you descend into the Hope Valley and head for Castleton and the Winnats Pass. It returns via Peak Forest and Tideswell. This route combines limestone and gritstone scenery with popular villages like Castleton and Eyam and the lesser known areas near Hathersage. It covers 52 miles (83km) and will take just over two hours to complete, excluding stops.

From Bakewell, take the A619 towards Baslow and turn left up the B6001 just past the Peak Park Joint Planning Board offices in Baslow Road. The B road continues on past the old Hassop Railway Station (now a bookstore), built for the Duke of Devonshire, and on to Hassop where the hall is now a fine restaurant and hotel. Turn left here, noting the classical style of the church's front on your right, and proceed through Great Longstone, turning right here at the T-junction in the village. There are some interesting houses in Great Longstone, especially the delightful hall behind the large gateposts on your right as you leave the village. Continue on through Little Longstone to Monsal Head with its

famous view of Monsal Dale and the old railway viaduct. Turn right along the B6465 to Wardlow Mires where the road reaches the A623. Turn right here and take the first turning to the left into Foolow village. The large green here still has a duck pond, old cross – albeit in a new position – and a bull-baiting stone situated adjacent to the cross.

From Foolow, turn right for Bretton and proceed directly ahead towards Eyam Edge. Climb up the steep hillside towards the Barrel Inn where there are fine views over the moors and southwards back towards Longstone Moor. Descend into Eyam village and turn left. Eyam is worth exploring for it is, of course, well known for its connections with the plague, but its churchyard also has a fine Celtic cross. From the village turn left for Hathersage, taking the B6521 and, when it reaches the main valley road between Calver and Grindleford, turn left for Grindleford. Cross the River Derwent and climb up through Nether Padley and into the plantations of the Longshaw Estate of the National Trust.

Longshaw Lodge will eventually come into view on your right and there is a National Trust information centre and tea room here. On reaching the A625, turn left for Hathersage. Ahead there are views to Carl Wark, the Iron Age fort and beyond towards the Hallam Moors and Stanage Edge. After about 1 mile (1.6km), the road goes through a cutting on Millstone Edge at a point well known as the Surprise View, and indeed what a surprise it is.

Beyond, the view extends right up into the Hope Valley with its high moors on either side. After half a mile (800m) or so beyond Surprise View there is a turning to the right. Take this minor road and after about 2 miles (3.2km) there is a turning to the left. Take the first right, signposted to Ladybower, and continue following the signs.

The road eventually descends to the A6013. It winds its way below the great expanse of Stanage Edge with marvellous views to the south-west and westwards towards Castleton. Upon reaching Yorkshire Bridge, turn left down the A6013 to meet the A625 near Bamford Station, although you might wish initially to turn right, ie westwards, through Thornhill to Castleton, but if you prefer to see Hathersage, proceed in the opposite direction down-river a couple of miles or so to make the necessary detour.

Castleton today is very much a tourist village with its caves and Norman castle. There are the usual gift shops, but here one may also buy Blue John stone, the unique decorative stone which is quarried south of Mam Tor just to the west of the village. The route from here proceeds towards the Caverns, then past Speedwell Cavern and up the Winnats Pass, the old turnpike road which carried the A625 under Mam Tor having been closed because of the repeated land slips as a result of the unstable hillside. After you have climbed up the impressive Winnats Pass, the road reaches the B6061. Turn left and, on reaching Sparrowpit, turn left across the front of the Wanted Inn for Peak Forest, on the A623.

Having gone through Peak Forest village, the main road bears sharply to the left and then again to the right. This short alignment of the road at 90° to the general run is, in fact, part of the old Roman road between Buxton and Brough, near Hope. Of perhaps more interest is Eldon Hole. If you look to the north at this point you can see a dark hole enclosed in a stone wall on the hillside of Eldon Hill. This enormous pot-hole drops vertically for over 170ft (52m).

Leaving Eldon Hole behind you, continue down the road and turn right for Tideswell. This village and its beautiful church are always well worth exploring. From Tideswell the route continues down the valley into Tideswell Dale, eventually passing Ravenstor Youth Hostel and descending into Miller's Dale, with its two impressive railway bridges that stand side by side. Having climbed out of the valley again, the road soon reaches the A6 Buxton-Bakewell road. Turn left for Bakewell and, having bypassed Taddington, the road descends down Taddington Dale to rejoin the River Wye and the run back to Bakewell. If you want a further detour into Ashford-in-the-Water, turn off at the appropriate sign.

The Northern Moors

This is a circular route that covers the bleak northern moors and the valleys and moorlands of the north-east side of the Peak District. The route is a circular one, which starts for convenience in Buxton. The route may be joined at any point whether you approach from the south, Manchester, Holmfirth or Sheffield. This route is rather long – 81 miles (130km) – and takes about three hours. It can be reduced by proceeding straight to Glossop from Buxton

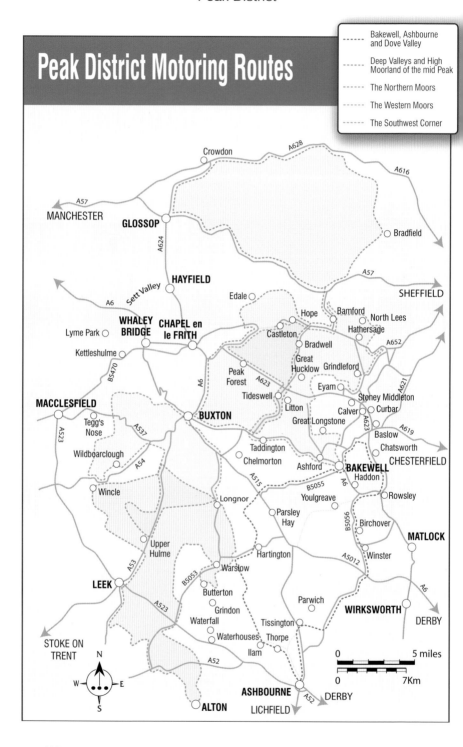

Peak District Motoring Routes

Legend:
- Bakewell, Ashbourne and Dove Valley
- Deep Valleys and High Moorland of the mid Peak
- The Northern Moors
- The Western Moors
- The Southwest Corner

The two former railway bridges at Miller's Dale

via Hayfield and also by following the signs to Strines and Derwent Valley from Langsett, leaving out the Bradfield area. If map reading is not your strength, the latter may be a good idea in any event.

From Buxton, take the A6 northwards through Dove Holes to the large bend at the southern end of Barr Moor Clough where the A623 leads off on the right to Castleton. Turn right here and look out for Bennetston Hall on the left, before you reach Sparrowpit and the Wanted Inn. Leave the A road here and continue down the left-hand side of the pub on the B6061 to Castleton. About 1 mile (1.6km) after you have passed Eldon Quarry, the Castleton road bears off to the right down Winnats Pass. Continue on the B6061 for a little longer before turning off to the left on the A625, taking the sharp turn to the right after about a quarter of a mile (400m) for Edale. The road

climbs up to Mam Nick with Mam Tor and its hill fort above you to the right.

Upon reaching Mam Nick, the Vale of Edale spreads before you with Kinder Scout clearly visible on the opposite side of the valley. The lane drops steeply down into the valley. On reaching the valley, the road bears to the right. After a while, turn left (signposted Edale only) and, after going under the railway bridge, look for the Peak Park Information Centre on the right, just before the church. From Edale, rejoin the valley road that runs down the Vale of Edale to Hope. It is a pleasant run but the road is narrow in places.

Upon reaching the T-junction in Hope, turn left along the A625 towards Hathersage. After 2.5 miles (4km) turn left again on the A6013 for Bamford and Ladybower Reservoirs. A few yards up this road on the left can be seen the old turnpike gateposts which formerly existed at nearby Mylor Bridge. They have been erected here by the Park Authority and an interpretation board is also provided. Upon reaching Ladybower, cross the Ladybower viaduct to reach a T-junction. Turn left onto the A57 and cross the Ashop viaduct before entering the Woodlands Valley with the arm of the reservoir below you. Immediately below the south side of Ashop viaduct stood the village of Ashopton. The road climbs the valley and up over the Snake Pass at 1,680ft (512m) before it drops down to Glossop.

In Glossop, take the B6105 to the right (by the Norfolk Arms). This road climbs out of the town and into Longdendale. It runs the length of Torside Reservoir before crossing the dam of Woodhead Reservoir to join the A628. Turn right and continue climbing up the Woodhead Pass on the A628 for several miles until you reach The Flouch Inn. Turn right on to the A616 (signposted Sheffield) for Langsett. Once in the village, turn right (signposted Strines and Derwent Valley) across the dam of Langsett Reservoir. Take the third road to the left to the small village of Bolsterstone. En route, a few junctions are not clearly marked, but turn right and head for the church tower in the distance. Pass through the village and keep the church on your right (notice the nearby stocks behind the railings). Descend the hill, ignoring the left turn to Ewden and soon Broomhead Reservoir is reached.

Cross the bridge at the end of the reservoir, then bear left and then second right up the hill through the wood. At the crossroads, go straight ahead and take the next right (with the West Nab transmitter on your right) to High Bradfield. You then descend to Low Bradfield. Bear right into Smithy Bridge Road and then left and climb up the hill past the Plough Inn. Turn right at the T-junction (signposted Ughill and Strines) and follow the road back to the A57 Glossop-Sheffield road. Look out for a tall tower, known as Boot's Folly, on your right and across the valley can be found the ancient Strines Inn.

At the A57 bear right for Ladybower Reservoir and take the A6013 through Bamford to the A625. Turn right and after 2 miles (3.2km), turn left on the B6049 through Brough, Bradwell, Tideswell and Miller's Dale to the A6, the Buxton-Bakewell road. Turn right here for the run back to Buxton through Ashford Dale.

The Western Moors

This route takes you from Buxton across the upper Dove Valley to the Roaches and on to Macclesfield Forest and the Goyt Valley. It covers some 45 miles (72km) and takes about two hours.

Leaving Buxton on the A515 to Ashbourne, the limestone quarries are soon reached. After about 3 miles (4.8km), turn right for Longnor on the B5053, crossing the River Dove at Glutton Bridge. Here may be found the nearest thing to 'peaks' in the Peak District – the rounded reef limestone hills that flank the River Dove.

Climbing up the valley, Longnor is soon reached. Turn right at the market place – it is signposted to the Royal Cottage and Leek – and cross the southern end of Axe Edge to Middle Hills and the A53 Buxton-Leek road. Turn left for Leek; you soon pass Ramshaw Rocks, with the bleak expanse of Morridge on your left. Descend the steep hill beyond Ramshaw Rocks and, near the bottom, turn right into Upper Hulme and then left. Pass the works and follow the road around, eventually past the large outcrop of the Roaches. Contour around until you reach Roach End, when you can pull off the road to admire the tremendous view. Ahead the landscape is dominated by Shutlingsloe rising to 1,659ft (505m). To the west, the high ground ends suddenly at Bosley Cloud where the land drops to the Cheshire plain. Here is some of the finest scenery in the Peak, which mercifully is not as popular as the northern and eastern moors.

The road continues around the back

of the Roaches. Incidentally, it goes through two gates before reaching a T-junction. Turn left here and then right before rejoining the A53 almost opposite the Winking Man pub, named after a rock on Ramshaw Rocks. Turn left up the A53 towards Buxton and 1.25 miles (2km) after the Traveller's Rest Inn turn sharp left, over a cattle grid and across Axe Edge Moor. Take this unfenced road to the A54 and turn left for just over 2 miles (3.2km). Upon reaching a plantation, turn right for Wildboar-clough and descend to the Clough Brook at the bottom of the road. Turn left for Allgreave (signposted Wincle) and upon reaching the A54 again, turn right for about 1.5 miles (2.4km) until you reach the Fourways Motel.

Turn right at this point and make your way uphill for Langley. To your left in the clump of trees is the medieval Cleulow Cross, a monastic guidestone. Keep to this narrow lane, eventually passing the Hanging Gate pub, with Shutlingsloe now to your right. Shortly after passing the pub, turn to the right on a bend and continue, gradually descending to the bottom of the hill where you turn left at a T-junction in Macclesfield Forest. Skirt around Ridgegate Reservoir and at the Leather's Smithy pub turn right uphill for Bottom-of-the-Oven and Forest Chapel, a simple church that still has an annual rush-bearing ceremony. At the next two T-junctions turn left and at the Stanley Arms turn left. Cross the A537 (signposted Goyt Valley) and descend to Lamaload Reservoir where there is a picnic area.

Beyond the water, bear right at the next junction and proceed to Jenkin Chapel, which was built in 1733.

Follow the road to the right and uphill to cross over Pym Chair and descend down into the Goyt Valley and the twin reservoirs of Fernilee (the lower one) and Errwood. There are picnic areas near Errwood Dam and near the other end of the lake where there are woodland trails to the ruins of Errwood Hall. This is a beautiful spot when the rhododendrons are in flower. To return to Buxton, cross Errwood Dam, climb the hill (this is part of the Cromford and High Peak Railway line) until it reaches the A5002. Turn right and you soon descend back into the town.

The South-west Corner

This route explores part of the beautiful Churnet Valley, the ridges and wild moorlands of North Staffordshire and part of the Dane Valley. A section of this route follows (in reverse) part of the Potteries and Moorlands Leisure Drive and should not be confused with this. It takes some 2.5 hours and covers 60 miles (96.5km).

From Leek, take the A520 south to Cheddleton. Look out for the Flint Mill on your right at the bridge, just before the road climbs up through the village. At the top of the hill, turn left down Basford Bridge Lane. Upon reaching the T-junction adjacent to the old Cheddleton Railway Station, turn right for Ipstones. Turn right after 1.25 miles (2km) (signposted 1.5 miles to Ipstones) and proceed by the quiet and wooded area that is adjacent to Belmont Pools. Look out for Chapel House Farm, converted from a former church, complete with its small tower and restored east window.

At Ipstones, turn right on the B5053 and, on reaching the A52 at Froghall, turn left (signposted to Ashbourne). If time permits, you can turn left after a few yards, on the Foxt road, to explore Froghall canal wharf where there are toilets and picnic area. On reaching Whiston on the A52, turn right opposite the Sneyd Arms for Oakamoor. This road runs along the northern side of the Churnet Valley before it descends into Oakamoor. Cross the rather long bridge over the River Churnet and then turn left down the very picturesque valley road to Alton. On reaching Alton, turn left over the elegant river bridge and climb out of the valley past Alton Towers.

Proceed through Farley with its fine looking hall and some pleasant sandstone cottages. This road reaches the B5317 at the Ye Old Blazing Star Inn. Turn right and after about a mile (1.6km) turn left (signposted to Winkhill and Leek). Cross the A52, over the next crossroads and then bear left immediately behind a white painted cottage and proceed along Ipstones Edge. On reaching the B5053, turn right for Bottom House where you cross the A523 and start to climb up the southern flank of Morridge on the road to Onecote. Take the first left and follow the ridge all the way to the Mermaid Inn. Turn right here, past the gliding club and over the moors to Warslow. Just beyond the Greyhound Inn turn right on the B5053 and take the road back towards Onecote.

Climb the hill after crossing the Warslow Brook and turn left for But-

terton. At the village, turn left and bear left at the church and then right in front of the school for Wetton Mill. The road heads for the delightful Manifold Valley. Descend into the valley and turn left along the old railway track. After going through the tunnel, bear right and left over the bridge following signs for Hulme End. The lane passes the old Ecton Copper Mine and eventually brings you to Hulme End. Turn right and then left for Sheen and Longnor, the road eventually running along the ridge between the valleys of the Dove and Manifold.

At Longnor market place, turn right for Buxton and then second left, just past the fire station, for Flash. This road continues the theme of travelling high along the ridge between the river valleys, which are now wider apart. Upon reaching the Buxton to Leek road (A53) at the Traveller's Rest Inn, turn left and first right into Flash, the highest village in England. This lane drops down into the Dane Valley to Gradbach and Allgreave. At the Rose and Crown Inn, at Allgreave, turn left on the A54 and, after crossing the river, turn left for Wincle. Although the road is narrow in places, you might like to stop and look around, if only to stand and admire the scenery. At Wincle, head for Swythamley via Danebridge, Meerbrook and then turn to Leek along the A53 again.

Finally, motorists would do well to avoid Ashbourne on summer Sunday and Bank Holiday evenings whenever possible. Even worse is the A6 either side of Matlock and Matlock Bath, which can be bypassed by taking the Wirksworth to Grangemill road and then the B5056 which leads to the A6 west of Rowsley.

9. Wildlife in the Peak

Cressbrook Dale

The Peak consists of a large number of different habitats, some of which are nationally important. The gritstone is covered in many places by moorland. Areas where public access exists, such as Kinder Scout and the Eastern Edges, offer many opportunities to explore some wonderful countryside. Even when access is denied to certain areas through conservation schemes (such as on Big Moor east of Froggatt or on The Roaches, north of Leek) or through private ownership as on Beeley Moor, it is often possible to enjoy views across it. In addition to the moors, which are covered with heather, bilberry bushes and cotton grass, several semi-natural oak woodlands survive. Some of these, such as Padley Wood, north-east of Grindleford and Jagger's Clough in the Vale of Edale, are also accessible. Here sessile oak survives in a habitat unchanged for thousands of years.

There is a variety of habitats on the limestone too, and many of these may be visited. From country lanes and footpaths one may see at first hand the upland grassland of the limestone plateau. The rare and acidic limestone heathlands can be seen from the convenience of the car south of Parsley Hay on the A515. Where the road crosses over the railway, there are banks of heather on the steep slopes above the old line. There can be no difficulty in distinguishing the large beds of heather, especially in September, when the blooms, a mass of bright purple in the sunlight, may be seen.

Grassland habitats can be seen in the dales from footpaths or on National Park land such as Tideswell Dale. Here one may see grassland flora amid the limestone outcrops at the northern end and lower down the dale; perhaps the best example is on the slope opposite the old quarry. So diverse are the habitats in the dales that English Nature has established the Derbyshire Dales National Nature Reserve, which is referred to in detail below. Without doubt, the abundance of flowers and plant life in the dales, augmented by rocky crags and crystal-clear streams, justifies their popularity. Here the potential for conflict arises from too many visitors to sites of special scientific interest (SSSI). Many visitors do not understand the sensitivity of the nature reserves or natural ashwoods, such as those at Dovedale and Lathkill Dale. They see the dales only as places of recreation.

The old railways allowed other habitats to develop too, and these may now be observed from the three trails opened by the National Park and the Manifold Valley track. Other unusual habitats are the old lead mine rakes, which cut across the fields. Now they are the home of lead-tolerant plants such as spring pennywort, the mountain pansy, and, on Bonsall Moor, the alpine pennycress.

The rich variety of wildlife in the Peak may be seen from many areas in public domain where visitors are encouraged. Many nature reserves also exist where public access allows visitors to view especially sensitive areas. The reserves are controlled by wildlife organisations who welcome casual, responsible visitors, as long as they keep to the rights of way, and they also welcome members. The remainder of this section is devoted to a description of these, sometimes little known, reserves.

Until the early years of the twentieth century, local farmers grazed their sheep on the steep sides of the dales. The result of this practice was that the tree and bush cover was far less than it is now, as seedling trees and bushes were eaten. Over the centuries, the short grassland developed a great diversity of plants, especially of the low-growing, rosette type of plant that survives sheep grazing. Farmers now find that it is no longer economic (or even reasonable, given the volume of visitors) to graze sheep on the steep valley sides. This has resulted in the growth of rowan, ash, sycamore, elder and especially hawthorn scrub, which gradually develops into woodland. Some hawthorn scrub is valuable for birds and insects, but when it starts to cover nationally famous, flower-rich grassland, control is necessary. Sycamore is also a problem, especially in ancient woodlands where its early and heavy shade, plus heavy leaf fall, reduces the variety of early flowering plants on the woodland floor.

The situation became so serious in Dovedale that the many natural rock features were hardly visible behind the foliage. The character of the relict ash wood began to change too, with the growth of the intrusive sycamore. The National Trust decided to restore the valley by the removal of the sycamore plus much scrub, including hawthorn and elder. The result is not only a pleasant surprise, but a valley which our forefathers would have recognised. These changes in the landscape are not as obvious as the changes made by man, which are often sudden and more drastic in comparison. Mindful of this, several nature reserves have been established around the Peak District aimed at conserving different habitats.

Some of these nature reserves are open to the public and others are open to members of the organisation responsible for the control of the reserve. The Derbyshire Wildlife Trust controls forty sites in Derbyshire, of which nearly fifty per cent are within, or fairly close to, the Peak District. Membership of the trust is recommended for those with a serious interest in the flora and fauna of the Peak. The position is further complicated because English Nature controls the Derbyshire Dales National Nature Reserve comprising the Lathkill, Monk's, Cressbrook, Biggin and Long Dales; Staffordshire County Council has opened a nature park at Consall in the Churnet Valley; and both the National Trust and the National Park own areas of land which are ecologically important. The National Park owns several large estates which are managed with nature conservation as a major objective. Most are open to the public but some have sanctuary areas because the wildlife is very vulnerable to disturbance.

Lathkill Dale

One of the most important sites is the 258 acre (104 hectare) National Nature Reserve in Lathkill Dale. It is described in detail here because it illustrates graphically how different the ecology can be over a small area. It also gives a good indication of what one may expect to find in similar locations in the other limestone dales. The dale is best approached from either Monyash or Over Haddon. At the head of the dale, which is not part of the reserve, where there is easy access to the sides of the valley, it has been easy for farmers to improve the land with lime and other fertilisers. Improvement is necessary because the limestone is porous along bedding planes and other fissures in the rock.

Flora

Consequently, the soil is leached of lime and other salts (making it slightly acidic) as the water carries the salts downwards. The pasture here is lush with introduced grasses and has little floral diversity. The farmers' activities were impeded in places because of the slope and rocky outcrops. Here the flora changes and includes maidenhair spleenwort, brittle bladder fern and winter annuals.

The character of the dale changes upon reaching the second field, for the slopes become much steeper and were therefore of less value to the farmer. Because the slopes were less amenable to improvement, the flora is much more diverse and includes, for example, meadow saxifrage and lady's smock. Further into the dale there is

169

an amazing diversity of habitats, with soils differing between the north and south-facing slopes. The latter have a greater daily temperature range with evaporation from the soil. This draws up the lime from the sub-soil and makes the surface soils rich in lime. This suits calcicole plants in abundance, as many as fifty species per square metre growing in some locations. The south-facing slopes, being warmer, also attract the sheep and such habitats favour short, often rosette-forming species, which the sheep find difficult to nibble.

Here may be found rock rose, salad burnet, quaking grass, mouse-ear hawkweed, bird's-foot trefoil and thyme. The ungrazed areas are dominated by tall grasses that provide cover and food for invertebrates and small mammals. A third habitat is found by the screes of fragmented limestone where herb robert, shining cranesbill and false oat grass are common. Nearer the woodlands, ash and dog's mercury take over.

The north-facing slopes are just the opposite, but not only in geographical terms. The moisture and less extreme climate variation creates a much lusher environment and therefore the plants tend to be taller, with such plants as dog's mercury, rosebay willow-herb and meadow cranesbill. It also includes perhaps the country's largest colony of Jacob's ladder, its deep blue flowers visible in June and July.

The more acidic soils support the heath bedstraw and also heather and bilberry. Although heather is not usually associated with limestone, the leaching process creates more acidic soils than we often appreciate and, where the soil is left untouched, conditions can often be appropriate. Consequently, there are more localities where heather may be seen than are realised and these are referred to below.

The lusher growth generates a greater leaf-litter and resultant deeper soils. It also reduces the plant diversity, excluding the smaller species. The reduction of grazing in the dale is therefore reducing the plant species. Work by Sheffield University has shown that there has been a drop from forty to twenty species per square metre over an eighteen-year period on land that is no longer grazed. English Nature believes that if regular and controlled grazing was introduced into the dale, especially on the north-facing slopes, an extremely interesting and diverse flora could result. The lack of grazing also encourages the development of scrub and tree cover, which English Nature has to control too.

Woodlands

Lower down the dale, the woodlands predominate. The Peak District ashwoods are probably the largest in Britain. The woodland has a good structured growth of trees from saplings to mature trees, especially those on the south bank. In medieval times the three monastic granges on the plateau above the river controlled the south bank and pastures above. It is probable that the monks would have made use of the timber, but would not have over-exploited it. Ash quickly regrows from the stumps and good management would have seen the replanting of trees to augment 'tired' stumps after prolonged coppicing.

Low Wood east of Cales Dale, and on land formerly belonging to Callinglow

Grange, is a good example and it is now one of the oldest natural elm/ash woods in the Peak District. Following the dissolution of the monasteries, the Cavendish family, now Dukes of Devonshire acquired the land and still own much of the land adjoining the dale. The system of careful woodland management continued much as before.

North of the river, much of the woodland disappeared because of lead mining and sheep grazing. After the closure of the mines (Mandale Mine closed in 1852), the area was replanted with a mixture of trees, including alien species such as sycamore, beech and Scots pine. The planting was actually carried out in two phases, with ash, beech and elm being planted in the Mandale Mine area in about 1870 and sycamore, ash, Scots pine and spruce being planted in the western end of the wood after the small mines in this area closed in about 1915. A section of the wood was felled during World War II and self-sown ash, sycamore and elm can now be seen growing here.

The unfelled area is now over-mature and careful management is allowing holes to be created in the leaf canopy. This in turn helps the natural regeneration of ash and other native species.

Fauna

The various habitats of the dale have an important bearing on the variety of both the bird and butterfly population. Butterflies often need different conditions and habitats at each stage in their life cycle. The reserve is fortunate in being able to support about twenty different species. Not only is the habitat important; disturbance from agriculture and other human activities can often prevent breeding. Here in the reserve, such problems are controlled.

The bird population similarly takes advantage of the different habitats. In the grassland, scrub and rocky outcrops of the western end of the dale, jackdaws are particularly noticeable. This area also supports the kestrel, little owl, meadow pipit, wheatear and pheasant. In the winter, redwing and fieldfare take advantage of the shelter and food, with huge flocks visible on occasions. In the summer months, warblers including the white throat, finches and thrushes can be seen.

The woodlands attract their own, different birds. Here the great-spotted and green woodpeckers live alongside the tree creeper, nuthatch and wood

Lathkill Dale Dilemma

A problem is that English Nature finds it impractical to own its own sheep flock. Clearly, the grazing needs to be controlled, for the taller grasslands despite creating an important habitat for invertebrates, small mammals and reptiles, prevent smaller plants from growing. Annual grazing licences granted to local farmers go some way to achieving the ideal situation sought by English Nature, but the best solution would be for them to own their own flock of sheep, with their own shepherds, but financial limitations restrict this.

warbler. The pine trees support the goldcrest, coal tit and sparrow hawk. Another predator of the woodland is the tawny owl, although it is often missed because of its nocturnal habits. One is also lucky to see the hawfinch, which tends to avoid contact with man. The river also has its own habitat. Here the dipper, grey wagtail, moorhen, little grebe and occasional mallard find a home. If one is lucky, a visiting kingfisher may be spotted together with the heron searching for fish.

The path through Lathkill Dale is very pleasant. The crystal-clear water of the river allows fish to be seen with ease – and there are some big ones, too. The path east of Carter's Mill is, however, a concessionary one only. In such a sensitive area as the reserve it is vital that care is taken to ensure that the wildlife is not disturbed. English Nature produces a variety of leaflets (some being on sale at the pathside near Lathkill Lodge) on different aspects of the reserve. It is important that this is done, because a greater understanding of why the dale is so ecologically sensitive will foster a greater protection of it by its users.

Monk's Dale

English Nature has an addition to its Derbyshire Dales National Nature Reserve at Monk's Dale, a tributary valley of the River Wye at Miller's Dale. There is a small extension of this in Peter Dale (actually an extension of the same dale), which gives a total area for the reserve of 149 acres (60 hectare).

The dale is cut into the limestone, similar to Lathkill Dale, but a major difference is that it has a north-south orientation and therefore lacks the climatic contrast of Lathkill Dale. A further contrast is that the woodland at Monk's Dale consists chiefly of ash but also includes much sycamore; rowan, whitebeam and bird cherry are absent from the wood. Consequently, the woodland is probably not as old, despite a rich ground flora that is typical of old woodland.

Although the soils of the upper edge of the dale have been leached, the flora supports small patches of sheep's fescue, common bent and bitter vetch. There is no development of limestone heathland with heather and bilberry, however. On the floor of the dale are a series of seepage zones and calcareous flushes with tufa in evidence. These flushes are more prevalent here than in other dales. Grass of Parnassus and bryophytes are characteristic of this habitat. English Nature is reducing the scrub cover and sycamores and ensuring that grazing continues. Thus the rich flora of the close-cropped limestone grassland is being maintained. A public footpath extends up the dale, but a permit is required if people wish to wander from this, which is usually granted only for scientific work.

Derbyshire Wildlife Trust

Among the reserves managed by the Derbyshire Wildlife Trust are several crossed by public rights of way. Details of these are given, but a permit is required to wander off the right of way.

Ladybower Wood

This 40 acre (16 hectare) reserve was purchased in 1976. A path runs north-east from the A57 beside the Ladybower Inn. Parking is difficult and cars should be parked at the south end of the viaduct across the eastern arm of Ladybower Reservoir on the A6013 to Bamford. A good view of the wood is obtained from this position.

The path runs along the southern border of the reserve, leaving it at the Nether Brook. The 15 acre (6 hectare) wood is a good example of a sessile oak woodland, which formerly covered much of the gritstone edges and moorlands. It has survived here because this area of difficult, steep and rocky terrain discouraged grazing. Among the oak can also be found birch and rowan, and coring suggests that the trees date from around 1865, after the area had been felled. The flora is characterised by wavy hair grass, heath bedstraw, bilberry, bracken and heather.

A large part of the site is covered by gritstone scree, including some areas of very large boulders. Here bilberry, heather and cowberry grow with large specimens on some ledges. The cliffs also support greater woodrush, violet, ivy, wood sage and honeysuckle.

Lichen is abundant, fifty-eight species having been recorded including several rare to Derbyshire. Thirty-two species of mosses and liverworts have also been recorded. There is a good bird population, with nearly forty recorded species including cuckoo, kestrel, woodcock, tawny owl, tree pipit, plus great, coal and blue tits, treecreeper, thrushes, redstart, warblers and, as one might expect, the ubiquitous jackdaw on the cliffs.

Ladybower Wood is within a Site of Special Scientific Interest (SSSI).

Opposite Ladybower Wood and visible from it, is Priddock Wood, tucked against the side of Bamford Moor. This wood does not have any rights of way across it, however. Here 36 acres (15 hectare) have been leased to create the reserve. It is another good example of sessile oak woodland with open heather moorland above. Among the bird population are red grouse and the ring ouzel.

Overdale Reserve

East of Bradwell is a further gritstone reserve occupying 45 acres (18 hectare) of land off Brough Lane at SK185805. It is an area of upland pasture, 1,000-1,250ft (305-381m) high, divided into three areas by two streams which cut across it. One stream occupies a steep-sided valley with a 10ft (3m) high waterfall. Part of the site is flat and the eastern stream often flows beneath the turf, creating a wet habitat. Over 100 species of flowering plants including 20 sedges and rushes have been recorded, plus 11 ferns, over 60 mosses and liverworts and about 30 lichens. Because the site is grazed, an area has been fenced off and in 1976-7, nearly 2,000 silver birch and sessile oak were planted.

Miller's Dale

There are three reserves near Miller's Dale village occupying three sites and 219 acres (89 hectare) south of the River Wye; these are Chee Dale, Miller's Dale Quarry and Priestcliffe Lees. All are graded as SSSI.

The Chee Dale site runs from Blackwell to the footbridge south of Wormhill and is visible from the riverside path and the Monsal Trail, as well as being crossed by two footpaths south-west of Black-well Cottages. The site is an outstanding example of ash woodland and limestone grassland. The wood includes elm, bird cherry, birch, whitebeam and yew along the cliff edges. The herb layer includes globe flower and lily of the valley. The western end is grazed and is rich in cowslips, salad burnet, spotted orchid, grass of Parnassus and moonwort.

The other sites, opposite the Angler's Rest Inn and Ravenstor Youth Hostel, support similar habitats with a rich flora that includes various orchids on the quarry floor. The steep slopes opposite Ravenstor include wood violets and both dark red and broad helleborine. Above the wood are the spoil heaps of old lead mines, now chiefly grassed over and supporting the yellow and purple mountain pansy, spring sandwort and

Birds and butterflies

By the River Wye, one may see the dipper, kingfisher and grey wagtail. In the woods above are found blackcap, wood warbler, chiffchaff, spotted flycatcher and green woodpecker. As with Lathkill Dale, the kestrel, jackdaws and house martins can be seen overhead, nesting on the cliffs. The butterfly population includes the small tortoiseshell, orangetip, brown argus, small heath, dingy skipper, large white, green veined white, small copper, common blue, red admiral, peacock, wall and meadow brown. In addition, over fifty species of moth are known.

Priestcliffe Lees

thyme. Paths cross the sites from the following access points: the roadbridge over the river; opposite the Angler's Rest public house; opposite Ravenstor Youth Hostel and opposite Litton Mill. The Monsal Trail forms the northern boundary of both Miller's Dale and Priestcliffe Lees Reserve.

Hillbridge Wood, Taxal

North-west of Buxton, halfway between Taxal and Fernilee Reservoir, lies Hillbridge Wood on the west bank of the River Goyt at SK010787. A footpath cuts diagonally across the site, climbing uphill from the footbridge over the river. This 12 acre (5 hectare) reserve is chiefly oak woodland with rhododendron beneath. The latter is being removed together with the sycamore to encourage natural regeneration. Holly, silver and hairy birch grow in profusion, with a typical ground flora that includes bluebell, wood anemone and bugle. Several rare species of lichen have been recorded, together with forty-four species of bird and eleven mammals.

Rose End Meadows

This 19 acre (8ha) site at SK292567 complements the upland grassland reserves on both limestone and millstone grit. It has a combination of grasslands, including some pasture with similarities to the limestone dales. Other meadows are more characteristic of lowland unimproved meadows, which are now rare in Derbyshire. The flora includes two plants rare to Derbyshire: the pyramidal orchid and the narrow-leaved bitter cress.

Derwentside

There are two reserves on the Cromford Canal. Derwentside reserve extends to 17.5 acres (7 hectare) in a linear strip south of the Wigwell Aqueduct, by Lea Wood Pumphouse. The reserve ends just south of Gregory's Tunnel and may be seen from the canal tow-path and the footpath at Homesford. The site originally became a reserve because of its wild daffodils in the woodland at the southern end, which is now fenced off so that the public cannot pick the flowers. However, the diversity of the flora is far greater than at first thought. Among the birds that have been recorded are the green woodpecker and the treecreeper, and eight butterfly species have been noted. Like the Cromford Canal site (below), the insects found here include rare hoverflies.

The 13 acre (5 hectare) Cromford Canal reserve, graded SSSI, consists of the canal and its banks, including the tow-path from Whatstandwell to Ambergate. Over 250 plant species have been recorded, together with over eighty species of hoverfly, several butterflies and also both dragonflies and damselflies. Frogs and toads breed in the canal, together with pike, which can often be seen basking at the water's edge. Grass snakes also frequent the canal banks. Over fifty bird species have been recorded.

The Trust has a further four sites on the northern Peak, at Long Clough, Broadhurst Edge Wood and Watford Lodge, all south-west of Glossop, plus Brockholes Wood at Crowden in the Longdendale Valley.

High Peak Trail

On the High Peak Trail there is a reserve at Longcliffe Cutting (SK235557), which is wooded rather than grassland. On one of the non-wooded slopes there is a population of alpine pennycress, which is unusual as it is normally associated with lead-mine spoil heaps, which are not present.

Further down the line at Hopton Tunnel Cutting (SK267548) is a 5 acre (2 hectare) reserve between the steepsided cutting. The Black Rocks Reserve (SK293558) consists of spoil heaps with a high lead concentration. Consequently the plants consist of lead-tolerant varieties such as alpine pennycress, and spring sandwort and moonwort, which are probably not lead tolerant, but which require an infertile soil to avoid competition with vigorous species. The tips are slowly becoming covered with grass and scrub and include the broad helleborine, which is generally uncommon in Derbyshire.

Other Railway Trail Reserves

The sections of the High Peak and Tissington Trails within the National Park are controlled by the Park Authority and treated as if they were one big 'reserve' from a conservation point of view.

The main habitat is grassland and rock outcrops. The flora is rich and typical of the limestone plateau grasslands, such as quaking grass, great burnet, cowslip, salad burnet, milkwort, purging flax, tway blade, lady's bedstraw, carline thistle and lady's mantle. Dropwort, which is not common in Derbyshire, occurs at the southern end of the reserve. As may be expected, several varieties of orchids, together with thyme, slender bedstraw and rockrose, grow on the thin soils of the rock outcrops.

Staffordshire Wildlife Trust

The Staffordshire Nature Conservation Trust has five reserves in the area and public access is available to four of them.

Castern Wood

This 51 acre (21 hectare) reserve (an SSSI since 1972) consists of deciduous woodland, scrub and grassland above the River Manifold. A public footpath runs along the top of the valley and the reserve is now open to the public with a path down into the wood. The area in which the reserve is situated is part of a complex series of lead mines, some of which are deep, one being 300ft (91m). It is approached down the narrow lane that runs south-east from Wetton to a rather high signpost where the road ends. A gate on the right leads to a track across the side of a field to a parking area. The upper valley consists of grassland, which is kept grazed. Much of the hillside consists of a mixture of ash, wych elm, sycamore and a few limes and field maple. There is a variety of birds and flowers and some interesting and rare beetles.

Brown End Quarry

South-west of Castern Wood is Waterhouses and an old limestone quarry rich in wildlife but particularly important for

Rare limestone heath

Of particular interest is the development of limestone heath, with heath bedstraw and large quantities of heather. This can easily be seen from the A515 at Parsley Hay and is one of several sites adjacent to the roadway where heather grows. Another good site is Alsop Moor Plantation, owned by the National Trust, where beds of heather may be seen without leaving your car.

its rich fossiliferous beds. These yielded a fossil new to science: Hampsancora brown-endensis. Special interpretative displays are provided giving detail on both the geology and the wildlife.

Coombes Valley

Between Waterhouses and Leek, some 4.5 miles (7.2km) from Brown End, a turn to the left (signposted RSPB Coombes Valley Reserve), over the railway line and up the side of a small hill, brings one to Six Oaks Farm, Apesford. Here is a reserve held jointly with the RSPB. The reserve is chiefly wooded with oak predominating. It has a rich bird life and diverse flora.

Baldstone

This reserve of 63 acres (25 hectare) is situated between the Roaches and Flash village, west of the Leek-Buxton road at SK018641. It is crossed by a public footpath and consists of mixed moorland and upland grassland on mill-

stone grit. It is an excellent habitat for moorland insects and birds, including thirty-three breeding birds.

The Churnet Valley

The park area totals some 230 acres (93 hectare) and consists of part of the Churnet Valley and the tributary Lady Park Valley. The area is also opposite Booth's Wood which, together with Rough Knipe and Crowgutter Woods, are managed by the RSPB as an extension of the Coombes Valley Nature Reserve. A considerable area is wooded, with additional areas of heathland, a small amount of farmland plus wetland habitats. The area has had a rich and varied industrial past, which even now is significant with its influence upon habitats.

It is an area where there is considerable opportunity to show the visitor much of the history and ecology. It does, however, have many sensitive habitats that require careful management. The area is, for instance, a location for the small pearl-bordered fritillary butterfly and the wood fescue grass, both of which are rare here. The park is reached by proceeding through Consall village, past Consall Old Hall to the Visitor Centre.

Cheshire Wildlife Trust

Danes Moss

Just to the west of the park and close to Gawsworth is an ancient 'raised peat moss' at SJ908704. The reserve extends to some 31 acres (12.5 hectare) and adjoins the Macclesfield to Stoke-on-

Heather on limestone heathland in railway cutting south of Parsley Hay

Trent railway line. A public footpath runs along the northern boundary and can be reached at SJ903701, on the Gawsworth to Fool's Nook road (off the A523 Macclesfield-Leek road). Some 10 acres (4 hectare) of the area has been flooded in order to reactivate peat formation. Access along the public path is available at all times; access away from the path, for reasons of safety, is by means of a permit. There is an unusually large population of willow warblers and at least seventy-five species of bird have been recorded. The areas of water attract wildfowl during winter and early spring.

Macclesfield Forest

The National Park Authority and North West Water have a joint Ranger Service at Macclesfield Forest. Various paths have been laid out, including a short one for disabled people at Trentabank Reservoir, which has the largest heronry in the Peak District, situated in the larch trees that line the eastern shore. There are, in fact, two reservoirs: Trentabank and Ridgegate.

Evidence of red deer may be found, although the animals themselves are rarely seen. The forest supports at least thirty different types of fungi as well as several woodland birds and wildfowl. A car park/information point exists near Trentabank Reservoir. The Cheshire Wildlife Trust controls a shore-line nature reserve with access limited to members.

Yorkshire Wildlife Trust

The Yorkshire Wildlife Trust has one nature reserve at Agden Bog. It is a reserve of only 6 acres (2.4 hectare) situated adjacent to Agden Reservoir in Bradfield Dale, 13km (8 miles) north-west of Sheffield. Unfortunately the bog is not crossed by a public right of way. Plant species include the more usual cotton grass, bilberries, cross-leaved heath, plus cranberry, bog asphodel and two insectivorous plants: sundew and butterwort. In addition, some forty species of birds have been recorded around the reservoir.

Getting to The Peak District

The Peak District lies in the centre of the country between the cities of Manchester, Sheffield, Stoke-on-Trent and Derby. Main roads cross the area from these cities and the motorways but there are very few dual carriageways in the Peak. Public transport is available to the area and offers a more relaxing way of arriving than coming by car.

Air

There are three airports close to the Peak District, Manchester being the closest:
Birmingham: www.bhx.com ☎ 08707 335511
Manchester: www.manchesterairport.co.uk ☎ 0161 489 3000
East Midlands: www.eastmidlandsairport.com ☎ 01332 852852

All have car hire facilities; there are stations at Birmingham and Manchester.

Bus

National Bus Travel Line ☎ 0870 6082608
National Express ☎ 0870 5808080 www.gobycoach.com
Regular coach services serve the surrounding areas and some travel into the Peak.

Train

National Rail Information

☎ 08457 484950 www.thetrainline.com
The following lines serve the Peak District: Derby to Matlock; Manchester to Buxton and Glossop; Manchester to Sheffield, via the Hope Valley

Accommodation

Lists of various types of accommodation may be obtained from tourist information offices. Lists are available from the Peak District National Park and the district councils of Staffordshire Moorlands, Derbyshire Dales and High Peak. (see Useful addresses)
There is a full range of serviced accommodation: hotels, guest houses, bed and breakfast establishments and farm houses; a wide variety of self-catering properties; caravan and camp sites.

Agencies

Derbyshire Dales Ashbourne Accommodation Group
☎ 01335 344795 www.ashbourne-accommodation.co.uk
Derbyshire Country Cottages
☎ 01629 583545 www.derbyshirecountrycottages.co.uk
Peak District Farm Holidays
☎ 0781 764 2627 www.peakdistrictfarmhols.co.uk
Peak Cottages
☎ 0114 262 0777 www.peakcottages.com
Chatsworth Estate
☎ 01629 565300 www.chatsworth.org/stay-with-us

Youth Hostels

There are fourteen youth hostels in the Peak District. You do not have to be a member to stay. It is advisable to book in advance to ensure a bed. Many of England's youth hostels have private rooms, with upgraded facilities. In the Peak, at both Castleton and Hartington, are rooms with ensuite facilities in a separate annexe. Several others have private rooms including Alstonfield, Ilam Hall, Edale, Gradbach and Matlock.
The YHA runs a Rent-a-Hostel scheme called escape to... which enables some hostels to be available in the winter season exclusively for private groups. This has proved to be very successful and you may have to book well in advance.

There are youth hostels at Alstonfield, Bretton, Castleton, Crowden, Dimmingsdale (Oakamoor), Edale, Eyam, Gradbach, Hartington, Hathersage, Ilam, Ravenstor near Miller's Dale, Sheen and Youlgreave.

Further details are available from: YHA Trevelyan House, Matlock, Derbyshire DE4 3YH

☎ 0870 770 8868 www.yha.org.uk

Camping Caravanning

There is a large number of sites for both tents and caravans. Details can be obtained from the Peak National Park and local tourist information offices.

☎ 0870 2255 450 www.visitpeakdistrict.com

Bird watching

Carsington Reservoir, near Wirksworth
Coombes Valley Reserve, south of Leek
Deep Hayes Country Park,near Cheddleton
Tittesworth Reservoir, north of Leek

Caving

The many caves and mines should never be entered by the inexperienced. Useful contacts are:
Peak District Mines Historical Society c/o Peak District Mining Museum, The Pavilion, Matlock Bath ☎ 01629 583834
Derbyshire Caving Club www.derbyscc.org.uk

Cave Rescue

In an emergncy dial 999 and ask for Cave Rescue.

Climbing

There are excellent gritstone crags at Stanage, Froggatt, Burbage and the Roaches. There is limestone climbing in the White Peak area such as Matlock Bath. For full details and access contact

The British Mountaineering Club: ☎ 0870 010 4878 www.thebmc.co.uk
There are indoor climbing walls at:
The Foundry: Sheffield ☎ 0114 279 6331 www.foundryclimbing.com
Upper Limits: Longnor ☎ 01298 83149

Cycle Hire

Carsington Water

Carsington, Nr Wirksworth
☎ 01629 540478
Open: Daily from 10am.
Cycle track around the reservoir

Derwent Reservoirs

Fairholmes
☎ 01433 651261
Open: Daily from Mar–mid-Oct. Weekends and half term the rest of the year.

Manifold Valley Light Railway Trail (Hamps & Manifold Valleys)

Hire centre in old railway goods shed at rear of the Crown Inn, Waterhouses. Cycles may be also hired from Brown End Farm at the entrance to the tarmac-surfaced track.

Waterhouses
Old Station car park
☎ 01538 308609
Open: Daily Jul–Sep. Weekends and half term in Feb–Apr and Oct. Nov–Jan by appointment.

Brown End Farm
☎ 01538 308313 www.users.zetnet.co.uk/BrownEndFarm
Open: Easter–Oct 9.30am–6.30pm. Rest of the year by arrangement.

Monsal Trail & Bakewell

Bakewell Cycle Hire
Station Yard, Bakewell
☎ 01629 814004
Sett Valley Trail

Hayfield
☎ 01633 746222
Open: Jul-Sep daily approx 9.30am–6pm, rest of year weekends and Bank Holidays.

Tissington & High Peak Trail

Bikes may be hired from both Ashbourne and Parsley Hay station sites. The latter is situated just north of the old Hartington Station. Also Middleton Top Engine House. There is usually no need to book except for parties.

Ashbourne
Mapleton Lane
☎ 01335 343156
Open: Daily from Mar–mid-Oct. Weekends and half term the rest of the year.

Middleton Top
Middleton-by-Wirksworth
☎ 01629 823204
Open: Daily Jun–mid-Sep. Weekends and half term in Feb–May, late Sep and Oct. Closed Nov–Jan.

Parsley Hay
On A515 Ashbourne-Buxton road
☎ 01298 84493
Open: Daily April to September. Weekends and half term in February, October and November. Closed December and January.

Peak Park Bike Bus

A new service is now available to make it possible to take your bicycle to the Peak District whilst travelling by bus, or to take a linear cycle ride within the area and return on the bus. Bikes are carried on a trailer behind the bus. It operates from Biddulph in Staffordshire, travelling to Ashbourne via the Manifold Visitor Centre, Hartington Old Station and Waterhouses. During the day it runs between the last four places and then returns to Biddulph at the end of the day. Full details are available on ☎ 01538 386888

Emergencies

In the event of an emergency ☎ 999 and ask for ambulance, fire or police as appropriate. The police will alert mountain cave rescue if necessary, members of the public should not contact them direct.

Events

There are many activities going on in the area and the list below includes the majority of those occurring annually. Some events occur over the end of one month and the beginning of the next and are listed twice. It is important to realise that there are many events which are not included but which may be of interest. Readily springing to mind are the occasional steaming days at Leawood Pump House, festivals at Haddon Hall; local village events such as church festivals; talks and organised rambles.

Early spring
New Year's Day Bridge Jump, Mappleton, Ashbourne 12noon
Ashbourne Shrovetide Football: Shrove Tuesday and Ash Wednesday
Flagg Races (High Peak Hunt Point to Point): Tuesday after Easter

May
Bamford Sheep Dog Trials
Castleton Garland Ceremony
Chatsworth Angling Fair
Chatsworth Horse Trials
Leek Arts Festival
Leek May Fair

June
Ashbourne Arts Festival
Chapel-en-le-Frith Carnival

July
Alport Love Feast
Ashbourne Highland Gathering
Bakewell Carnival
Buxton Carnival
Buxton Festival
Glossop Carnival
International Gilbert & Sullivan Festival
Leek Show
Padley Pilgrimage

August
Ashbourne Show

continued on p.184

Gardens in and around the Peak

The area is blessed with some lovely gardens that are well worth visiting.

Biddulph Grange, between Biddulph and Congleton, north of Stoke on Trent, is a large Italianate Renaissance house of the 1840s. Now divided into up-market apartments, the gardens had become derelict, but were acquired by the National Trust in 1988. The Trust has restored the Chinese-theme garden to its original glory and a visit should be near the top of your priority list.

Nearby offering a contrast is the smaller and much older garden at the National Trust timber-framed **Little Moreton Hall**.

Parkland-type of gardens may be found at other National Trust houses, **Kedleston Hall** and **Sudbury Hall**, north west of Derby and south of Ashbourne, respectively.

Another landscape garden recently opened is at **Consall Hall**, south of Leek. With its carefully designed vista's, this has been a well-kept secret for far too long. If you are keen on rhododendrons, over 500 species flower at **Lea Rhododendron Gardens**, east of Cromford between spring and the end of July. Commenced in the 1920s, many species are now mature specimens in a woodland setting. Much newer, but also in woodland – this time a small valley – is **Dunge Valley Garden** near Whaley Bridge.

To the west, near Macclesfield is the National Trust's **Hare Hill Garden**, a haven of peace and quiet. There are rhododendron walks, a woodland walk and a walled garden to be explored.

Other gardens of size include **Renishaw Hall**, near the M1 and the one at **Alton Towers**. This has been too expensive to visit, as it is part of the theme park, but there are plans to provide access to the garden itself and it is well worth seeing if this happens.

For snowdrops, visit **Hopton Hall** or (taking a trip in to Nottinghamshire out of the Peak, visit **Oddsock Garden** near the junction of the M1 & M18. There are hundreds of thousands of them!

Lyme Hall, Disley will appeal to many ladies as this is where Colin Firth, as Mr D'arcy, emerged from the lake in BBC's version of *Pride & Prejudice*. It also has a sunken garden, camelia house and walk which takes in the lake!

Getting There:

Biddulph Grange: take the A527 from Congleton to Biddulph and look for the turn to the left that brings you to the right turn into the garden

Kedleston Hall: at Kirk Langley on the A52 between Ashbourne and Derby turn left and follow the signs

Sudbury Hall: take the A515 south of Ashbourne to Sudbury (under the A50) and at the roundabout, 2nd left into the village

Consall Hall: take the A520 south from Leek. Bear left at Wetley Rocks on the A522 and then first left to Consall. Turn left in village, passed the hall gates on your right (private), to the entrance after a further half-mile or so

Lea Rhododendron Gardens: at Cromford, take Mill Lane (also known as Mill road) to Lea. Turn left through Smedley's textile mill (it is both sides of the road; climb the hill and on bend to the right, turn right as signposted

Dunge Bottom: From Whaley Bridge take the Macclesfield road, B5470 and look for the sign to the left after going through Kettleshulme

Hare Hill: On the A538 Prestbury–Wilmslow road, 1/4 mile out of Prestbury, take left turn

Lyme Hall: from Disley, north west of Buxton, take the A6 towards Stockport and look out for the sharp left turn into the drive to Lyme Hall.

Sudbury Hall

Hare Hill

Dunge Valley Garden

Ashover Show
Bakewell Show
Bakewell Arts Festival
Chatsworth Country Fair (sometimes September)
Crich Tramway Museum, Grand Transport Extravaganza
Dovedale Sheepdog Trials
Eyam, Plague Sunday
Glossop Victorian Weekend
Hope Show
Ipstones Show
Macclesfield Forest Chapel Rush Bearing
Manifold Valley Show
Matlock Bath Illuminations

September

Hayfield Sheepdog Trials and Country Show
Longshaw Sheepdog Trials
Matlock Bath Illuminations and Firework Display

November

Castleton Christmas Lights
Christmas at Chatsworth

December

Castleton Christmas Lights
Christmas at Chatsworth
Peak Rail Santa Specials
Crich Tramway Village Santa Specials
Boxing Day Raft Race, Matlock Bath

Facilities for the Disabled

All places open to the public have to make their premises as accessible as possible to all members of the public. However there are some visitor attractions, such as stately homes, open-air attractions etc where complete access is not possible. No attempt to detail facilities has been made in this book as there are frequent changes. Please contact the individual attraction by telephone or look on their website to get up-to-date information.

In addition the Peak District National Park Authority produces a free booklet Access for All. Designed for disabled people, the less active and those with small children it gives details of nearly 90 sites in the Park including information on stiles, gates, rough and uneven surfaces, special toilets and public transport. Copies are available from the **National Park Offfice** at Aldern House, Bakewell, DE45 1AE, ☎ 01629 816302, or on-line at www.peakdistrict.org . An audiotape version is available on loan. See also places to visit pages of this book.

Fishing

Fly fishing

Certain hotels have rights available for guests. These include:

Baslow, Cavendish Hotel
☎ 01246 582311
River Wye: three rods, Cressbrook Mill to Ashford (approx 4.5 miles).
River Derwent: three rods, Calver Bridge, east side, and St Mary's Wood, west side, down to Smelting Mill Bridge, Rowsley (6.5 miles).
Brown trout are restocked annually from Chatsworth's ponds, rainbow trout and grayling breed naturally.

Dovedale, Izaak Walton Hotel
☎ 01335 350555

Matlock Bath, The Midland Hotel
☎ 01629 582630
River Derwent from Hall Leys Park, Matlock to Cromford.

Rowsley, Grouse & Claret
☎ 01629 733233

Peacock Hotel
☎ 01629 733518
Trout: 7 miles of River Wye.
Grayling: 2 miles of River Derwent.
Reservoir Fishing
For permission to fish the area's reservoirs contact the appropriate water authority.
Derwent Reservoir, Ladybower Reservoir

Fisheries Office, Ladybower
☎ 01433 651254

Tittesworth Reservoir
Meerbrook, Nr Leek
☎ 01538 300389

Damflask Reservoir
Loxley Valley, Nr Low Bradfield
Day tickets available at reservoir

Rudyard Lake
Rudyard, Nr Leek
☎ 01538 33280

Errwood Reservoir
Goyt Valley, Nr Buxton
☎ 01663 742168

Ogston Reservoir
Nr Chesterfield
☎ 01246 590413

Carsington Water
Near Wirksworth
☎ 01629 540478

Golf

A useful website that gives details of golf clubs in the area is www.uk-golfguide.com
Contact numbers for a selection of local courses are given below.

Ashbourne
18 holes
☎ 01335 342078

Chapel-en-le-Frith
18 holes
☎ 01298 812118

Bakewell
9 holes
☎ 01629 812307

Matlock
18 holes
☎ 01629 582191

Buxton and High Peak
18 holes
☎ 01298 23453

Guided Walks

The **National Park Rangers** offer a wide-ranging programme of guided walks throughout the year.
A full list is available in the free official newspaper of the Peak District to be found in information
centres and many other outlets. Information can also be found on the 24 hour walks information line
☎ 01629 816327.
The **National Trust** offer guided walks. Contact East Midlands Regional Office for details
☎ 01909 486411.
Staffordshire Moorlands Contryside Service run guided walks.
☎ 01538 483577 www.staffsmoorlands.gov.uk/services
English Nature run guided walks in the Peak District.
☎ 01629 816640 www.English-nature.org.uk/news

Maps

For walking and cycling the Ordnance Survey 1:25,000 Explorer Maps are recommended as
follows: 258 Stoke-on-Trent and Newcastle-under-Lyme, 259 Derby, OL24 The Peak District
– White Peak Area, OL1 The Peak District – Dark Peak Area. Motorists may prefer to use the OS
1: 50,000 Landranger maps, in which case nos. 109, 110, 118, 119, 127 and 128 will cover the
area. There is also an OS 1:100,000 Touring Map, Peak District and Derbyshire.
Harvey Superwalker Maps have a 1:25,000 Dark Peak. Goldeneye produce a laminated touring
map of the Peak District in 1:126,720 scale and a Cycling Routes map for the Peak District at
the same scale.

Markets

Market Days

Ashbourne: Thu and Sat
Bakewell: Mon (and cattle)
Buxton: Tue and Sat
Cheadle: Tue, Fri and Sat
Chesterfield: Mon, Thu (flea market), Fri
and Sat
Glossop: Thu, Fri and Sat
Leek: Wed, Fri and Sat.
Matlock: Tue and Fri
Wirksworth: Tue

Farmers' Markets

Bakewell: Last Saturday of the month
except Dec when it is the last Sat before
Christmas
Buxton: First Thu of the month (except Jan
& Aug)
Chesterfield: Second Thur of the month
Matlock & Leek: Third Sat

Public Transport

Travelline: ☎ 0871 2002233 for all public transport info
www.traveline.org.uk
There are bus services along most of the major roads across or around the Peak District, and the local authorities and the Peak Park Authority are making great efforts to encourage more local services in the area to make the Park a pleasanter place to visit. So, leave the car at home or in a car park outside the Park and travel by bus or train. Derbyshire County Council produces three comprehensive guides to all public transport in the area – Mid and South Derbyshire, Peak District and North East Derbyshire. They can be obtained from **Public Transport Unit, Derbyshire County Council**, FREEPOST, County Hall Matlock, DE4 9BR price £1.20 including p&p or from many libraries, TICs and shops in the area.
The only cross-Peak railway line is between Manchester and Sheffield along the Hope Valley line, with stations at Disley, Chinley, Edale, Hope, Bamford, Hathersage and Grindleford. Trains also run from Manchester to both Buxton and Glossop, and from Derby to Matlock, stopping at stations en route. It is also possible to make use of Peak Rail services between Matlock and Rowsley and it is hoped that within the near future there will be services from Duffield to Wirksworth.
To make it more economical to use public transport there are two tickets available that give unlimited access for a day's travel in the area:
Derbyshire Wayfarer Offers unlimited access to all buses and trains in Derbyshire and to the following surrounding towns and cities: Sheffield, Macclesfield, Leek, Uttoxeter, Derby and Burton-on-Trent, for a whole day. It also offers discounts to some Peak District attractions on the day on production of the ticket.
Family Freedom Ticket The Peak Bus Network operates on Sundays and Bank Holiday Mondays throughout the area and offers very economic fares for a day travelling on the bus network. There is also a **Hope Valley Family Freedom Ticket** just for the area of the Hope Valley and this is even cheaper.
All details of services and the special tickets can be obtained from ☎ 0870 608 2608 or www.derbybus.net

Riding Stables

Curbar Riding and Trekking Stables
Curbar, near Baslow
☎ 01433 630584

Haddon House Stables
Over Haddon, near Bakewell
☎ 01629 813723
www.tychetwo.co.uk/Edwin

Northfield Farm Riding and Trekking Centre
Flash, near Buxton
☎ 01298 22543

Red House Stables
Old Road, Darley Dale
☎ 01629 733583

Tissington Trekking Centre
Tissington Wood Farm, near Ashbourne
☎ 01335 350276

Sailing

Where sailing is allowed on reservoirs the relevant water authority has delegated responsibility for the sailing on that water to various clubs. In some cases these clubs allow casual visitors and it is necessary to write to the club if you wish to sail there.
Carsington Sailing Club
Carsington Water, Ashbourne
☎ 01629 540609

Squash Courts

There are squash courts at Ashbourne; Callow Park, Wirksworth; Leek; Glossop; Sheffield; and Cressbrook Mill, Monsal Dale.

Swimming Pools

There are pools at Leek, Cheadle, Ashbourne, Wirksworth, Bakewell, Buxton, Glossop, Matlock and Chesterfield, plus an open-air swimming pool at Hathersage with heated and filtered water, open May to mid-September (closed Sunday).

Tourist Information Centres

Ashbourne
DE6 1EU
☎ 01335 343666
ashbourneinfo@derbyshiredales.gov.uk

Bakewell
DE45 1DS
☎ 01629 816558
bakewell@peakdistrict.gov.uk

Buxton
SK17 6XN
☎ 01298 25106
tourism@highpeak.gov.uk

Castleton
S33 8WN
☎ 01629 816558
castleton@peakdistrict.gov.uk

Edale (The Moorland Centre)
S33 7HA
☎ 01433 670207
edale@peakdistrict.gov.uk

Hayfield
SK22 2ES
☎ 01663 746222

Upper Derwent Valley
S33 0AQ
☎ 01433 650953

Leek
ST13 5HH
☎ 01538 483741
tourism.services@staffsmoorlands.gov.uk

Matlock
DE4 3AT
☎ 01629 583388
matlockinfo@derbyshiredales.gov.uk

New Mills
SK22 3BN
☎ 01663 746904

Useful addresses

Peak District National Park Authority
Head Office, Aldern House
Baslow Road
Bakewell, DE45 1AE
☎ 01629 816200
www.peakdistrict.org
aldern@peakdistrict-npa.gov.uk
The National Park also run a wide range of residential courses at Losehill Hall. For details write to:

Peak National Park
Study Centre
Losehill Hall
Castleton
Derbys S30 2WB
☎ 01433 620373
leisure.losehill@peakdistrict-npa.gov.uk

National Trust
East Midlands Regional Office
Clumber Stableyard
Worksop
Notts S80 3BE
☎ 01909 486411
www.nationaltrust.org.uk

Derbyshire Wildlife Trust
East Mill
Belper
DE56 1XH
☎ 01773 881188
www.derbyshirewildlifetrust.org.uk

Staffordshire Wildlife Trust
The Wolseley Centre
Wolseley Bridge
Stafford, ST17 0WT
☎ 01889 880100
www.staffs.wildlife.org.uk

Friends of the Peak District
The Stables
22a Endcliffe Crescent
Sheffield, S10 3EF
☎ 0114 266 5822
info@friendsofthepeak.org.uk

RSPB
☎ 01767 680551
www.rspb.org.uk

Walking

Walking is the most popular outdoor activity as the Peak District has walks of all grades of difficulty and length, in fascinating and varied scenery. Many walks are described in this book, or plan your own route with the aid of a large scale OS map. Wear boots or stout shoes (especially on the moors), take weatherproof clothing and a map and compass (and know how to read them correctly).

Walking Trails

Probably the most famous of all long-distance walks in the UK is the **Pennine Way** and this starts in the Peak District. It runs 251 miles (404km) from Edale to Kirk Yetholm in Scotland and is a very challenging walk. Other trails within the Peak District are:

Derwent Valley Heritage Trail
Ladybower to mouth of the Derwent at Shardlow 55 miles (89km)

The Gritstone Trail
Disley to Kidsgrove 35 miles (56km)

The Limestone Way
Matlock to Castleton 26 miles (42km)

Midshires Way
Passes through the Peak District, runs from the Chilterns to Stockport 225miles (362km)

White Peak Way
Circular walk from Bakewell 81 miles (130km)
There are also several disused railway lines that are now walking/cycling trails. These are suitable for day walks and can also be used as a whole or in part, within a circular walk:

High Peak Trail Hurdlow to Cromford
Longdendale Trail Dunford Bridge to Hadfield
Manifold Valley Trail Hulme End to Waterhouses
Monsal Trail Haddon Park to Topley Pike
Sett Valley Trail Hayfield to New Mills
Tissington Trail Ashbourne to Parsley Hay

Walking Holidays

Walking holidays in the area are offered by the following:
Ramblers Association
☎ 01707 331133
www.ramblersholidays.co.uk

PDNPA at Losehill Hall
☎ 01433 620373

Peakland Walking Holidays
☎ 01298 872801
www.walkingholidays.org.uk

Free guide walks

Pick up a leaflet of National Park Ranger Guided walks or ☎ 01629 816200 (National Park H.Q.) or www.peakdistrict.gov.uk

Weather

For an up-to-date local forecast ☎ 09003 444 900 (premium rate)

Well Dressing

For a full list of Well Dressing dates, visit www.visitpeakdistrict.com

May

Endon, Middleton-by-Youlgreave, Monyash, Wirksworth
Tissington: Ascension Day until following Monday

June

Ashford-in-the-Water, Bakewell, Chelmorton, Cressbrook, Hope, Mayfield, Rowsley, Litton, Tideswell, Whaley Bridge, Youlgreave

July

Belper, Bonsall, Buxton, Buxworth, Chapel-en-le-Frith, Hathersage, Hayfield, Little Longstone, Peak Forest, Pilsley, Stoney Middleton

August

Barlow, Bradwell, Eyam, Foolow, Great Hucklow, Holymoorside, Taddington, Wardlow, Wormhill

September

Chesterfield, Hartington, Longnor
If you would like to see a demonstration of the well dressing art a number of places, such as those below, offer the opportunity prior to the actual dressing of the wells. Contact the local TIC for exact times and dates.
Buxton, Eyam, Hope, Litton, Longnor, Middleton-by-Youlgreave, Monyash, Stoney Middleton, Taddington, Tissington, Wardlow, Wormhill

Index

Published in the UK by:
Horizon Editions Ltd
Trading as The Horizon Press,
The Oaks, Moor Farm Road West, Ashbourne, Derbyshire DE6 1HD
E-mail office@horizonpress.co.uk

4th Edition

ISBN 978-1-84306-492-3

© **Lindsey Porter 2010**

British Library Cataloguing in Publication Data:
A catalogue record for this book is available from the British Library

Printed by: Gomer Press Limited. Llandysul, Ceredigion, Wales
Cartography and Design: Mark Titterton
Edited by: Ian Howe

Picture Credits:

Front cover: Losehill (Visit Peak District)
Back Cover top: Wetton
Back Cover bottom: Chatsworth House
Title page: Foolow

Paul Deakin: 119all
Derbyshire Wildlife Trust: 174
Ron Duggins: 103 both
Trustees of Chatsworth Settlement: 150 bottom
Mark Titterton: 2, 7 top, 10, 14 top, 22 top left, 22 bottom, 34, 51 both, 54, 63,
66 bottom, 79 top, 90, 94, 98, 131 top
Visit Peak District: 6, 39 bottom left, 62, 66 top, 86, 87, 90, 102 both, 122 top right &
bottom, 123, 126 top, 134,135 bottom, 139 both, 139 bottom, 154, 155, 167,
front cover. See www.visitpeakdistrict.com
Stella Porter: 122 bottom
All other photographs are supplied by the author

DISCLAIMER
While every care has been taken to ensure that the information in this guide
is as accurate as possible at the time of publication, the publisher and author
accept no responsibility for any loss, injury or inconvenience sustained by
anyone using this book. Please note that some attractions may open slightly
differently either side of winter. Also that times may vary.